Photo by: Chelsie Hutto

Tribute to Paula Ramsey
"Mom"

Paula Ramsey, founder & owner of "A Lady's Day Out" has gone to be with her sweet savior. On August 22, 2000 she lost her battle with cancer. Mom's life was an example for many. We can all be assured her rewards were great and that the Father welcomed her home with open arms and a big "Thank you" for a life spent glorifying Him and bringing many into the Kingdom.

"A Lady's Day Out" was Mom's vision. As with most things in her life, she was willing to share this with me. We traveled from one exciting town to the next—finding treasures and experiencing so much together for more than 10 years. I was blessed to have shared these times with my mom and hold them dear in the quiet places of my heart.

The loss of my best friend, business partner and mother is great, and the pain is deep. Our family has lost our "rock," but our faith in the Lord is strong, and we take comfort in knowing we will someday join her again in heaven.

I will miss our adventures together, but I am thankful for the times we shared, and I feel blessed to have had a mom that others could only dream of. I have always been and will continue to be proud of my mother for her love of the Lord, her right choices, her ability to lead by example and the contributions she made here on earth. Mom had an unconditional love for all of her children, and as her daughter, I will miss that attribute the most.

We will continue to publish "A Lady's Day Out" books and see her vision through. A percentage of all book sales will go to charity in Mom's memory. Thank you for celebrating her memory with us. Each time you pick up this book or any of our others, we hope you think of Mom and her inspiration—Jesus Christ.

Jennifer "Jenni" Ramsey

The Faye Snodgrass Gallery

(See related story page 194.)

Southern Rhapsody

(See related story page 203.)

Photo by Chuck Jones

Bodyworks Emporium
(See related story page 223.)

Lillie Belles of Franklin
(See related story page 204.)

IV

Northgate Gallery, Inc. *(See related story page 94.)*

V

Bell Buckle Chamber of Commerce
(See related story page 85.)

Bell Buckle
Pottery
*(See related story
page 89.)*

ReCreations
(See related story page 26.)

Hardin County Tennessee

Get Away To It All

Hardin County
(See related stories page 255.)

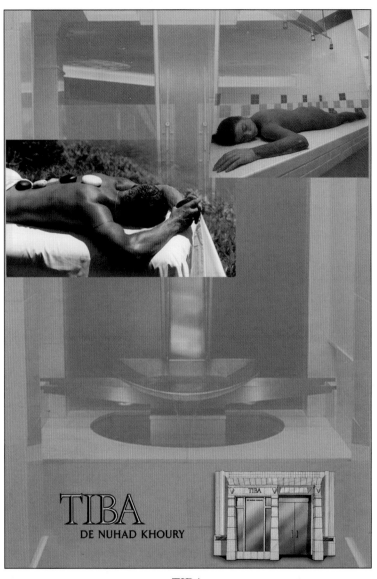

TIBA
Spa, Perfumery, Accessories, Gifts, & Fine Jewelry
(See related stories pages 40 & 55.)

Photo by Tracy Knauss

Cumberland County Playhouse
(See related story page 134.)

Courtyard Marriott
(See related story page 79.)

Circa Home Interiors LLC
(See related story page 191.)

Mayfield Walker
Galleries
(See related story page 183.)

Baymont Inn & Suites
(See related story page 222.)

Jack Daniel's Visitor Center
(See related stories pages 164 & 167.)

Staff Photography

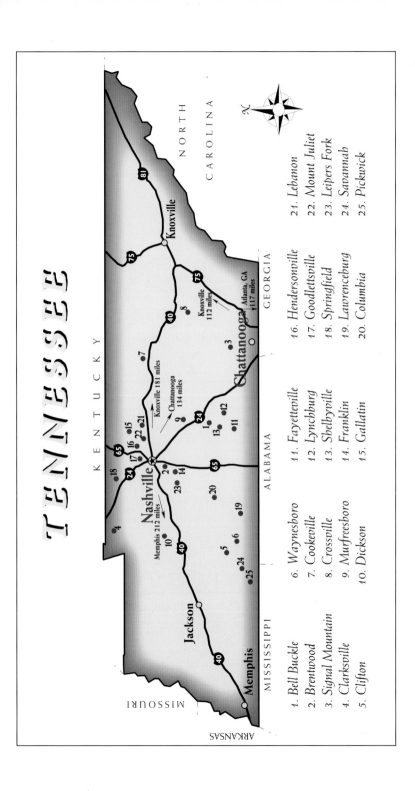

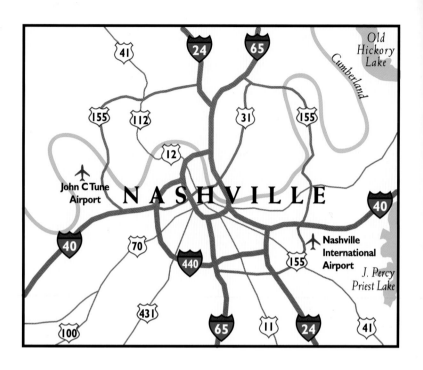

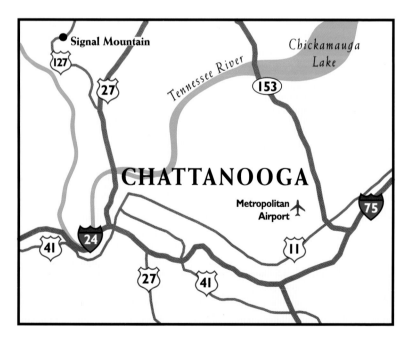

Available Titles

After enjoying this book, we are sure you will also love our other books:

"A LADY'S DAY OUT ON NORTHWEST FLORIDA'S EMERALD COAST"

Sparkling, emerald green waters along miles of pristine sugar white sand beaches make the Emerald Coast breathtaking! You'll find beachside restaurants, shopping treasures, relaxing accommodations and sun-kissed attractions among the unhurried world along the Gulf. This book is the perfect companion guide to adventurers exploring the warmth and hospitality of Apalachicola, Carillon Beach, Destin, Fort Walton Beach, Grayton Beach, Gulf Breeze, Mexico Beach, Navarre Beach, Niceville, Pace, Panama City Beach, Pensacola, Pensacola Beach, Port St. Joe, Rosemary Beach, Sandestin, Santa Rosa Beach, Seagrove Beach, Seaside, Shalimar and Valparaiso. — *237 Pages - $19.95*

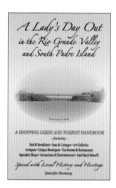

"A LADY'S DAY OUT IN THE RIO GRAND VALLEY AND SOUTH PADRE ISLAND"

Discover why the Rio Grand Valley and South Padre Island are the perfect places for a "two-nation vacation"! With one set of roots planted deeply in Mexico, and the other firmly in Texas, this book is loaded with magnetic "Beinvenidos" appeal. Tourists from the Northern United States flood to the Valley during the winter months to enjoy the warmer temperatures and delightful lifestyle. Vibrant shopping, casual eateries, charming attractions and wonderful accommodations makes this book a must have when planning an afternoon, weekend or week long get-away in Alamo City, Brownsville, Edinburg, Harlingen, Hidalgo, La Feria, Los Fresnos, McAllen, Mission, Pharr, Port Isabel, Port Mansfield, Raymondville, Reynosa, Rio Grande City, Roma, South Padre Island, and Weslaco. — *176 Pages - $19.95*

"A LADY'S DAY OUT IN THE TEXAS HILL COUNTRY, VOLUME II"

Spiced with local history and Heritage; this book is our latest edition for the Texas Hill Country. Featuring the best bed & breakfasts, inns, cottages, art galleries, antiques, tea rooms, restaurants, unique boutiques, specialty shops, attractions and entertainment the Hill Country has to offer. Find out why the Texas Hill Country is a favorite destination for all. Plan your trip by using this book and you'll be sure to guide yourself to the best and most unique towns and shops the Hill Country has to offer. Featuring the wonderful towns of Bandera, Boerne, Medina, Vanderpool, Blanco, Brady, Brownwood, Early, Burnet, Buchanan Dam, Comfort, Fredericksburg, Goldwaite, Hamilton, Johnson City, Stonewall, Junction, Kerrville, Ingram, Lampasas, Llano, Marble Falls, Kingsland, Mason and Wimberley. — *250 - Pages - $18.95*

"A LADY'S DAY OUT IN MISSISSIPPI"

Southern charm and uniqueness drip from the pages of this Shopping Guide and Tourist Handbook. We have found true Mississippi treasures! As always great shopping, dining and lodging fill the pages of this book in this fascinating state. Bay St. Louis, Biloxi, Canton, Cleveland, Columbus, Jackson, Natchez, Ocean Springs, Oxford, Pass Christian, Picayune, Vicksburg and Waveland are all covered. — *212 Pages - $17.95*

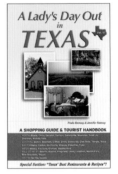

"A LADY'S DAY OUT IN TEXAS, VOL. III"

Features 37 new "GET-A-WAY" Texas towns—most are new and not covered in Texas, Vol. II—brimming with fascinating history and delightful, unique shopping. Inside you'll find all the details about romantic bed & breakfasts and inns, fabulous antique shops, lovely art galleries, home décor, gift shops and exciting entertainment, tea rooms, soda fountains and much more. — *276 Pages - $18.95*

"A LADY'S DAY OUT IN TEXAS, VOL. II"

Let us guide you through the highways and by-ways of Texas through 27 HISTORIC TOWNS & CITIES. True to form we have found the best shopping, dining, bed & breakfasts and inns in great, not so well known "GET-A-WAYS."
346 Pages - $17.95

"A Kids Day Out in the Dallas-Fort Worth Metroplex"

A book to plan an entire childhood, not just a day, private schools, sports, dance, art, entertainment, pets, stables, fun dining and more. — *214 Pages - $16.95*

— BOOKS SOON TO BE AVAILABLE —

"A Lady's Day Out in Dallas, Vol. II"
"A Lady's Day Out in Atlanta, Georgia & Surrounding Areas"
"A Lady's Day Out in Northern New Mexico"

Book Order Form

A Lady's Day Out, Inc.
8563 Boat Club Road
Fort Worth, Tx 76179
Toll Free: 1-888-860-ALDO (2536)

Please send me _____ copies of **A LADY'S DAY OUT IN NASHVILLE, CHATTANOOGA & SURROUNDING AREAS** at $19.95 per copy, plus $2.00 postage for each book ordered. (Tax included.)

Please send me _____ copies of **A LADY'S DAY OUT ON FLORIDA'S NORTHWEST EMERALD COAST** at $19.95 per copy, plus $2.00 postage for each book ordered. (Tax included.)

Please send me _____ copies of **A LADY'S DAY OUT IN THE RIO GRANDE VALLEY & SOUTH PADRE** at $17.95 per copy, plus $2.00 postage for each book ordered. (Tax included.)

Please send me _____ copies of **A LADY'S DAY OUT IN THE TEXAS HILL COUNTRY, VOL. II** at $18.95 per copy, plus $2.00 postage for each book ordered. (Tax included.)

Please send me _____ copies of **A LADY'S DAY OUT IN MISSISSIPPI** at $17.95 per copy, plus $2.00 postage for each book ordered. (Tax included.)

Please send me _____ copies of **A LADY'S DAY OUT IN TEXAS VOL. III** at $18.95 per copy, plus $2.00 postage for each book ordered. (Tax included.)

Please send me _____ copies of **A LADY'S DAY OUT IN TEXAS VOL. II** at $17.95 per copy, plus $2.00 postage for each book ordered. (Tax included.)

Please send me _____ copies of **A KID'S DAY OUT IN THE DALLAS/ FORT WORTH METROPLEX, VOL. I** at $16.95 per copy, plus $2.00 postage for each book ordered. (Tax included.)

MAIL BOOKS TO:

NAME: _____

ADDRESS: _____

CITY_____ STATE_____ ZIP_____

AMOUNT ENCLOSED: _____
CREDIT CARD ORDERS CALL: 1-888-860-ALDO (2536)

A Lady's Day Out

in

Nashville, Chattanooga & Surrounding Areas

A Shopping Guide & Tourist Handbook

— featuring —

Bell Buckle • Brentwood • Chattanooga • Clarksville
Clifton • Cookeville • Crossville • Dickson • Fayetteville
Franklin • Gallatin • Goodlettsville •Hendersonville
Lawrenceburg • Lebanon • Leipers Fork • Lynchburg
Murfreesboro • Nashville • Pickwick • Savannah
Shelbyville • Signal Mountain • Waynesboro

by Jennifer Ramsey

Cover features Gaylord Opryland Resort & Convention
(See related story on page 43.)

CREDITS

Editor/Author
Jennifer Ramsey

Director of Research & Sales
Jennifer Ramsey
Nena Prejean

Administrative & Production
Kay Payne
Mary Manzano
Beth Poulsen
Laura Pender

Editor & Writer
Michelle Medlock Adams

Research & Sales
Jennifer Stierwalt
Kendall Corder
Tere Carter
Chris Jewell
Courtney Isbel
Mandi Gaskin
Stacey Ligon
Todd Childs

Contributing Writers
Jenny Harper Nahoum
Gena Maselli
Jill Boyce
Gayle Norris

Table of Contents

Note from the Author

Well, A Lady's Day Out has ventured into another new state—Tennessee. I am so excited to share with you all the "Treasures" we found from Nashville to Chattanooga. I know you will love this state as much as we do. Most of you know that I have a tendency to measure how wonderful a state is by comparing it to my home state of Texas, and those are some pretty big boots to fill. However, Tennessee is pretty wonderful. From Nashville to Chattanooga, Tennessee ranks right up there with the best. More men from Tennessee died in The Alamo than any other state, so the ties between Texas and Tennessee are strong.

In this book, you will find charming, warm, friendly people, as well as sophisticated, cultured ones with businesses that reflect their character and uniqueness.

If you enjoy Tennessee as much as we did, you might be having just a little too much fun. Go ahead—enjoy!

Jennifer "Jenni" Ramsey

DISCOVER MIDDLE TENNESSEE

It is a place filled with magnificent natural wonders, exciting musical opportunities, fun-filled entertainment attractions, and people as warm and welcoming as a freshly baked apple pie. This verdant part of the Volunteer State called Middle Tennessee awaits you with her arms wide open and her guitars tuned. As you travel through Tennessee, you will notice that the people will introduce themselves as East, West, or Middle Tennesseans. This is because the state is so different from one region to the next.

The earliest evidence of man in Tennessee dates back 15,000 years, but the Native American "Mound Builders" are believed to have settled the area only 1,000 years ago. They built huge mounds—some five to seven stories high. Many of Tennessee's first pioneer settlers originated from North Carolina, because Tennessee was once part of this English colony. After the Revolutionary War, Tennessee remained part of the State of North Carolina until 1796, when Congress admitted it as the 16th state of the United States.

For thousands of years, the Cherokee lived in the Smoky Mountains of Middle Tennessee, but when white settlers began arriving during the late 1700s, the Cherokee were forced to leave. Soldiers marched them to the "Oklahoma Indian Territory," on what is known as the "Trail of Tears." It was named this because so many of the Native Americans died during this journey. Today, the Trail is a major tourist attraction. The Cherokee influence still remains throughout the area. In fact, the name "Smoky Mountains" came from a Cherokee word "Shagonigei" which means, "blue smoke." If you have never stood on a lookout point and watched the hauntingly beautiful blue smoke cover the Smoky Mountains, you are in for a wonderful treat. The entire countryside puts on quite a Technicolor show. The vivid colors of Middle Tennessee are breathtaking —the blue mountains, the rolling green hills dotted with wildflowers, the orchards of delicate apple blossoms, thousands of wild pink azaleas and purple mountain laurels, and the snow-white froth of the waterfalls. The scenery is almost too incredible to describe.

By the 1860s, the North and South had chosen two very different ways of life and philosophies about slavery. This same issue divided the State of Tennessee, and both sides experienced the devastation of war. Throughout Middle Tennessee you'll see the evidence of a place that has experienced the cruelties of war yet found a way to use its part in history to build a promising future. You'll see this in the wounded, but renovated plantation homes that dot the countryside; in the cemeteries that hold the remains of valiant Southern heroes; and in the grassroots traditions and values of the citizens.

Middle Tennessee draws millions of visitors each year. They come to take in the sights and sounds of Music City USA; to enjoy the famous Opry houses and dance halls; to tour the Walking Horse farms and apple orchards; to bask in the beautiful views of the mist-covered Smokies; and to explore the quaint wedding chapels and tucked away fishing cabins. From Chattanooga's famous Incline Railway (the world's steepest passenger railroad) and the swinging bridge over Lover's Leap to the world's largest freshwater aquarium and glass-bottom boat rides—you'll find it all here! Whether you like dark scary caves or prefer to tour lovely museums, Middle Tennessee is your perfect vacation spot.

The most famous city of this part of Tennessee is, of course, Nashville. It is called Music City USA, the Athens of the South, and the Buckle of the Bible Belt. It is a place that dances to an electric beat, yet is known as a world-class center for education and the arts. (Bring your camera and stay alert, because quite a few famous country singers call Nashville home!)

Although music might be Middle Tennessee's claim to fame, we know you will agree that her people are the number one attraction to the area. They are hard working, creative, honest people whose natural, easy-going personalities seem to fit so perfectly with their beautiful surroundings. They are hospitable, friendly and they simply love visitors. Don't be surprised if you are invited in for coffee and apple pie—it's just "the way of the South." So pack your bags, bring your husband and children, your appetite and your shopping lists, your camera and your dancing shoes, and discover the toe-tapping excitement of Middle Tennessee. Raise the curtain, IT'S SHOWTIME!

SPECIAL PEOPLE WHO CALL MIDDLE TENNESSEE HOME

Dolly Parton, one of the best known and most loved country singers in the world, was born in the Appalachian mountains, but moved to Nashville in 1967 when she landed a job on the popular Porter Wagoner Show. Famous for her big hair, big voice, and big heart (not to mention her impossibly curvaceous figure), Dolly Parton has become a beloved Tennessee treasure, whose voice resonates with the charm and hospitality that *is* the South.

The "tall drink of water" **Alan Jackson**, whose ride to fame was paved not with gold, but with hard work, determination, and true Southern grit, has sold more than 40 million records, and garnered more than 80 major industry awards. His songs touch a place in our hearts and evoke memories of the important events in our lives. Fans love this long, tall Southerner whose humble beginnings and old-fashioned values shine through in every performance.

Martina McBride's emerald eyes are as green as the beautiful countryside and sparkle with the passion and personality that have made her one of Nashville's most beloved daughters. Martina is recognized as the leading female vocalist in country music, but is also called, "the voice of the common woman." She continually uses her beautiful voice and incredible energy as the national spokeswoman for the victims of domestic violence, working with such programs as the Safe Haven Family Shelter. McBride was recently given the Grammy organization's highest honor, "The Heroes Award."

It is said of **Amy Grant,** "If you want to know Amy Grant's story, all you really have to do is listen to her songs." From the time she was a teenager singing for friends, until now when her albums rack up multi-platinum awards, Amy has always used her music to express her strong faith in God. Her career has spanned several decades, from Contemporary Christian to Pop/Rock, and her fans have loved it all. She is married to country music legend Vince Gill, and, of course, they call Nashville "home."

Vince Gill has walked away with 15 Grammys, and was inducted into the Grand Ole Opry. This laid-back, "Southern boy" feels just as natural picking bluegrass with his friends backstage as he does hosting the CMA awards, which he has done since 1992.

Another very beautiful and very famous Nashville couple continues to set records and claim awards in the country music business. Faith Hill and Tim McGraw are Tennessee locals whose careers seem to know no limits.

Faith Hill moved to Nashville at the age of 19, and never looked back or slowed her pace as she climbed the entertainment ladder to the top. Faith has been one of the industry's most remarkable and most successful (not to mention most beautiful) country music stars, selling 30 million records worldwide with 13 #1 songs and 18 #1 videos.

Tim McGraw says that he moved to Nashville "With little more than a wing and a prayer." Evidently, he also had quite a bit of talent, because he wasted no time at all in establishing himself as one of the most popular and loved country music performers in the industry. He has won almost every award possible in the music business, but says, "I look at it as a challenge to dig my heels in and keep getting better." He has!

The Judds, legendary country music mother and daughter phenomenon skyrocketed to fame in 1984 with their first hit, "Mama He's Crazy," and have maintained their incredible star-status popularity with their fans through the years. Mother Naomi and daughter Wynonna have been named two of the "40 Greatest Women of Country Music" by CMT—#11 on the list! When Wynonna mentioned her favorite Tennessee town in an interview, the place was swarmed with visitors hoping to find one of their favorite entertainers "at home."

She is known as "The Coal Miner's Daughter," and is called the "Queen of Country Music." **Loretta Lynn** has been country music's sweetheart for more than four decades and can count 52 top hits and 16 #1 songs. Her "rags-to-riches" life story is told in displays honoring her family, home-life, ranch life and musical career at The Coal Miner's Daughter Museum, which is located on Loretta's Plantation Home, Ranch, and Western Town just a few miles from Nashville. You might even find her puttering around the place, "trying to fix just one more thing!"

TENNESSEE TREASURES
—ITS PEOPLE

As you travel the luscious green hills and valleys of Middle Tennessee, explore the many historic Civil War battlefields, tap your toes to a hillbilly, country tune, or browse the many wonderful shops and eateries along the way, one thing will be constant throughout your visit—the remarkable genuineness and friendliness of the people. From the humble country moms and pops in the small rural towns to the glitzy, movie stars and award-winning musicians in the famous music houses and theaters, these folks are hospitable. There truly is something special about these wonderful Tennessee folks, who tip their hats as they drive by, always have a welcoming smile on their faces, and really say the words, "ya'll come back."

Because Nashville holds the honor of being the "Music City USA," it has attracted celebrities and musicians from around the world, and many have chosen the city as their home. But Nashville has plenty of "born and bred" natives who have left their distinctive marks on the area, as well. Tennessee is not only home to the world's best musicians, but also to world-class business and educational leaders. We know you will recognize a few of these famous Tennesseans, and maybe even get a chance to meet them during your visit.

DR. THOMAS FRIST, JR.

The Frist family is one of the most influential and respected families in Nashville, and is credited with having a significant impact on the health delivery system throughout the entire country. Dr. Thomas Frist, Sr., a gifted cardiologist, along with his son Dr.

Thomas Frist, Jr., and the late Jack C. Massey, founded HCA—one of the leading providers of healthcare services in the country. Dr. Frist, Jr., who is now Chairman Emeritus of HCA, served as its Chairman and CEO for 20 years. He is also chairman of The Frist Foundation, Nashville's largest charitable foundation.

This famous Nashville son received his bachelor's degree at Vanderbilt University and his M.D. from Washington University School of Medicine. His contributions to this city, state, and nation have been numerous. Among his many philanthropic endeavors was the founding of the United Way of America's Alexis de Tocqueville Leadership Giving Program in 1983 that has raised over $2 billion nationwide. As a testament to the incredible vision of this man and his family, The Frist Center for the Visual Arts opened in April 2001 in downtown Nashville. The project took more than seven years to complete, and it's the culmination of a community's long-awaited dream. Dr. Frist, Jr., said, "When my family and I thought of how important a new visual arts center would be for the people of Middle Tennessee, and when its development became a community-wide goal, we were excited to bring government and civic leaders together to help move the project forward and make it a reality. Art has meant so much to our own lives, and we want others to have the opportunity to experience the enrichment and enjoyment that the visual arts can bring to their lives too."

The center is 24,000 square feet of display space for visual arts presentations, including national and international exhibits. It is located within Nashville's historic post office building, which has been carefully renovated and transformed into the remarkable, state-of-the-art exhibition center.

Physician, philanthropist, businessman, visionary—Dr. Thomas Frist, Jr., has been the impetus of tremendous growth and development in the world of medicine, and a major contributor to the advancement of the arts in Nashville.

SENATOR BILL FRIST, MD

As the son of one of Nashville's most prominent and influential businessmen and physicians (Dr. Thomas Frist, Sr.), Senator Bill Frist continues his father's "Legacy of Leadership" as Senator for the great state of Tennessee. Dr. Frist was first elected to the U.S.

Senate on November 8, 1994, and recently elected to a second term by the largest vote ever received for a statewide election in Tennessee history. He was also the first practicing physician elected to the Senate since 1928. The Frists' family roots are planted very deeply in Tennessee history. In fact, Senator Frist's great, great grandfather was one of Chattanooga's 53 original settlers.

Senator Bill Frist graduated from Princeton in 1974, and with honors from Harvard Medical School in 1978. When he joined the faculty at Vanderbilt University Medical Center, he directed the multi-disciplinary Vanderbilt Transplant Center, which became a nationally-renowned center of multi-organ transplantation.

One of Senator Frist's passions has always been confronting the global issue of AIDS, and he has been on numerous mission trips to Africa to perform surgery and care for those in need. Even now, as the Senate Majority Leader, he continues his efforts to raise AIDS awareness throughout the world. Senator Frist was unanimously elected chairman of the National Republican Senatorial Committee, and currently serves on the Foreign Relations, Budget, Banking, Commerce, and Small Business committees.

Senator Frist, his wife Karyn, and their three sons are very active in their church and Nashville's community interests, but when the Senator has free time, he also enjoys flying, marathon running, and writing. He is an inspiration to those who know him; a blessing to his constituents in the political arena; a treasure to his community where he is an avid supporter of the arts; an angel in the matters of healthcare issues, bio-medical research, and organ donations; but most of all, his is a joy to his family, who look to him as a role model of a Godly man. We salute you, Senator Bill Frist!

GOVERNOR WINFIELD C. DUNN

Winfield C. Dunn was elected the 43rd governor of Tennessee in 1970—at that time the first republican governor to be elected in 50 years. Following his service in state government, he served as a member of the Board of Directors and Senior Vice President for Public Affairs for the Hospital Corporation of America. He has also served as a member of the Advisory Committee to the Director of the National Institutes of Health. As governor he was instrumental in the creation of a statewide public kindergarten program, the creation of the Department of Economic and Community Development and the reorganization of state government administration. Governor Dunn was named "Tennessee's Man of the Year" three times by the state's newspaper editors, television news directors, and heads of Chambers of Commerce. Winfield Dunn, however, says that his greatest "claim to fame" is his wife Betty Pritchard Dunn, a Memphis girl who captured his heart during their years at the University of Mississippi and introduced him to her beautiful state of Tennessee.

These two beloved Tennesseans have accomplished great things during their lives together, but they consider it all insignificant compared to their greatest joy in life—their three fine children and seven remarkable grandchildren!

Governor and Mrs. Dunn make their home in Nashville, and are active members of the First Presbyterian Church of Nashville. They list their loves as grandchildren, gardening, and golf. Winfield and Betty Dunn continue to amaze the community with the incredible gifts of their time and service, and remain two of the most respected and beloved people in Tennessee.

CAL TURNER, JR.

The name Cal Turner, Jr. is recognized throughout Tennessee as one of the state's most respected and honored businessmen. And, even if you are not familiar with his name, you will at once recognize the name of his business, Dollar General. The success of Dollar General stores throughout the United States has been phenomenal—more than 7,000 stores in 27 states. It is the largest chain of general merchandise stores in the country. Mr. Turner is chairman of the Cal Turner Family Foundation, and the retired Chairman and CEO of Dollar General Corporation.

When Mr. Turner's father and grandfather began working as dry goods wholesalers in 1939, the company was called J.L. Turner and Son. At the time of its initial public offering in 1968, the company changed its name to Dollar General Corporation. Dollar General enjoyed great success in the 1990s as a Fortune 500 Company.

Ask Mr. Turner about his success, and this humble, Christian man will always give the credit to his Savior, Jesus Christ. In fact, his life has always been one rooted in his strong Christian beliefs. He says, "I had a great family, but I was also adopted by a lot of

Sunday School teachers, a lot of ministers, and many teachers." He graduated from Vanderbilt in 1962, and then joined the Navy where he served for three years. Afterwards, he laughingly says that he "decided to accept the awful role of boss' son and come into the family business in 1965."

Mr. Turner recounts a funny story about choosing his college. When his father observed that he was looking at colleges in far away locations, his reaction was, "Son, I respect a man who makes up his own mind, and I want you to go to college anywhere you want to go. However, I will *pay* your way to Vanderbilt." Vanderbilt it was!

The Turners' family life was always about business. For example, the Turner children were asked to "pray for snow when the company was overstocked on overshoes, and, at other times, they were asked to pray for the snow to *melt* so that customers could get out to shop." Because the concept of family and business was so "co-mingled," the Turners learned the importance of offering this personal concept to their customers. They learned to pay attention to the needs and abilities of their customers who were usually low and fixed-income people struggling to make ends meet. Not only does Dollar General offer low-income families a place to find goods at prices they can manage, but the corporation also provides training and jobs for more than 1,500 low-income people—people who have the courageous determination to break the bonds of government dependence and get off welfare. Mr. Turner says, "Service to others is the business of Dollar General."

Cal Turner, Jr., spent almost 38 years as the head of Dollar General. Since his retirement in 2002, he has enjoyed the opportunity for contribution through philanthropy and mentorship to others who aspire to employ Christian management principles. It has been a time for creative reflection as to how God could use him to help others. Mr. Turner says that he hopes his talents and resources will be used to serve God, and that he has been honored to support various initiatives that are directed toward Christian leadership. He has supported many charitable organizations throughout the years and has endowed a chair in Wesleyan Studies at Vanderbilt University in Nashville. Mr. Turner was inducted into the Society of John Wesley in 2001 by the General Commission of United Methodist Men.

Cal Turner, Jr., has been an incredible witness in the business world, showing how Christian leaders can mightily change the course of lives; how Christian morals and ethics can be the basis for success; and how putting God first creates a beautiful "filter-down" concept of love that truly impacts a community and the world. In an interview with UMG.org, the official online ministry of the United Methodist Church, Mr. Turner said, "I hope that my life can help others to be inspired to serve God, not to take themselves too seriously, to have a sense of humor, especially when times get tough, and to have the inner assurance that the victory, the eventual victory of our Lord, is assured. No matter how things appear to us at the time, no matter how much defeat or hell is our plight at any given moment of life, God's gonna win. I'd like to be a part of that. And I want others to feel the challenge of that while I'm alive and after I'm gone."

MARTHA (MARTY) HALE

You might find Martha Hale leading a bus of tourists through the beautiful Tennessee hills or you might find her in the pulpit of one of two United Methodist Churches where she serves as minister. You might even catch a glimpse of her roaring by with her husband on a giant Honda motorcycle. You will *not* find her at rest! This incredible Tennessee woman runs at "get-it-done" speed. And, she has never met a stranger.

For many years, Martha worked with the Cumberland County Playhouse as Director of Group Sales. She worked to bring large out-of-state groups to the Playhouse to enjoy the world-class performances in Crossville, Tennessee. She left the Playhouse in 1996 to establish her own company called E.T.C. Tours—Experience the Cumberlands. Her tour company is extremely successful and one of the main contributors to the enormous growth of tourism throughout the Cumberland area.

Martha is the perfect tour guide because she is a sixth generation Tennessean. In fact, her family owns a 1,000-acre farm in a beautiful little valley called Grassy Cove. Her own farmhouse sits just 300 yards from her great, great grandfather's original homestead. Her family was one of the first families to settle in Grassy Cove in 1805, and the entire valley was named a National Natural Landmark because of the unique geological land formations of the area. Martha told us that most of the people in Grassy Cove today are the direct descendants of the first settlers who began to arrive here in 1801. History tells us that these first settlers named the area for the beautiful green grasses that were so tall they waved as high as the heads of the horses. There are few outside families here today, mainly because the farms continue to be handed down to generations who want to carry on the traditions of their forefathers.

On one of Martha's tours you will see the oldest church in the county, The United Methodist Church, which was established in 1803. You'll also discover one of her family's general stores, the J.C. Kemmer Store, which was established in 1886. In fact, she sums it up beautifully: You'll see one church, two general stores, lots of red barns, lots of old farmhouses, cattle, horses, and lots of friendly people. Her "step-on" tours might take you to the Grassy Cove Academy and the original Presbyterian Subscription School that was built during the 1800s, as well as the local cemetery where she will recant the amazing and famous "Petrified Confederate Soldier Ghost Story!"

Her clients include every type of group from Lifetime Learners to Boy Scouts, and they are all thoroughly entertained. Martha has a wonderful way with people. She is a United Methodist Minister who serves two churches here in the Crossville/Grassy Cove area. Her genuine love of God and His beautiful creation is evident in her pride of this wonderful area and its history. When she is not leading tours through the countryside, or ministering to the country folk in her church, she sometimes straps on her helmet and hops on a huge Honda motorcycle behind her husband John. Together, they explore the beautiful mountains and valleys of this incredibly beautiful area of Middle Tennessee.

"Experience the Cumberland" with Martha Hale. You will love her quick wit, her amazing story-telling ability, her first hand knowledge of the county's history, and the Christian, Southern hospitality she so beautifully personifies. You may call her Martha (Marty to all who knew her in high school); you may call her Reverend; you may even call her a "Motorcycle Mama;" and we're sure you'll call her friend. We're also sure you will not find anyone who enjoys life and people more than Martha Hale, from Grassy Cove, Tennessee! For information about ETC Tours you may call her at 931-484-0207 or email her at grassycovetour@multipro.com online.

MILLER LEONARD

We met the most remarkable woman while visiting Crossville, Tennessee, and in the process, learned a beautiful story of a lovely theater. Miller Leonard is the Creative Director/Writer/Producer of Advertising, Public Relations and Marketing for the Cumberland County Playhouse. She is a nationally honored executive with an outstanding resumé and a mile-long list of honors and achievements. She is bright, creative, successful, and hard-working, yet very humble. In fact, when we contacted her about this story, she wanted to tell *us* a story she thought would be much more interesting and exciting. She wanted us to know the incredible story of Paul and Mary Crabtree and their son Jim, who have led this little theater in rural Tennessee to almost unprecedented success.

A Divine Connection

The Cumberland County Playhouse in Crossville has an amazing genesis and the story is indeed, as they say in Hollywood, "the stuff dreams are made of." It reads like a wonderful Hollywood movie, and will probably make its way to the big screen one day. (Especially if Miller has her way!) It is amazing that so often wonderful people find other wonderful people. When Jim Crabtree met Miller Leonard, they both knew they were a perfect fit professionally.

Miller is North Carolina bred, born, and educated. She attended Sullins College and Vanderbilt University, and graduated from the University of North Carolina at Chapel Hill. She has been cited as one of the seven top copywriters in the Southeast, honored Top Ten in the nation by *Advertising Age* and was one of six finalists for a Clio award in radio, outdoor and print. Miller won the Presidential Award for Private Sector Initiative, numerous first-place Addy Awards, and has been awarded 33 Diamond Awards over the years for television, radio, print and outdoor. The list goes on and on and on! You will recognize many of her former clients from Dollar General Corporation and John Deere Parts and Service, to Aladdin Industries, Paul Harvey, Viacom, and the YMCA. She has also represented Easter Seals, the Cystic Fibrosis Foundation, and Stanley All-Steel Thermos.

She was President and Creative Director of Goodrum Leonard Associates, Inc., from 1989-1993, and then established Miller Leonard Creative Services, Inc., which she still operates on a freelance basis. It is no surprise that Jim at once recognized that Miller Leonard would be an incredible asset as the Creative Director of the Playhouse. One of the greatest benefits to having Miller on board is her pride in the Cumberland County Playhouse, as evidenced by her insistence that we hear the wonderful story of Paul and Mary Crabtree and their generous gift to this city.

The Story Behind the Story

Paul and Mary Crabtree met in 1943 while touring with the musical "Kiss and Tell" by George Abbot—one of the most famous directors in Broadway history. Paul was invited by Mr. Rodgers and Mr. Hammerstein to appear in "Oklahoma" on Broadway, and he was cast by Eugene O'Neill in the "Ice Man Cometh." He wrote for, acted with, and directed legendary Broadway stars, and both Paul and Mary did summer stock. It was during this time that Mary took on her most challenging and most rewarding role—mother to seven children! The family moved to Los Angeles where Paul wrote scripts for favorites such as "Bonanza," "The Loretta Young Show," and many others that are syndicated today.

In 1965, the Crabtrees (all nine of them) came to Crossville for the summer. Mary's great grandfather had helped found the town, and she had spent many summers there as a child with her grandparents. She wanted her own children to have that same experience. During their summer vacation, Paul wrote a little play called "The Perils of Pinocchio" and invited every interested child in the town to perform. It was such a tremendous success that an idea began to form in the minds of "powers that be." The Crabtrees' summer vacation turned into a lifetime of memories when they were approached with the idea of remaining in Crossville to help bring true theater to Cumberland County. At that time, the town's population was listed as 5,000, and access to the larger cities was grueling. However, people began to hear of the incredible talent and wonderful quality of the performances in Crossville, and they came from everywhere to be enchanted by The Cumberland County Playhouse.

The Show Must Go On...

Paul Crabtree died in 1979, but the theater has continued to flourish under the management of Mary and now their son Jim, who is a Yale Drama School graduate. Jim has directed his mother Mary in many plays including "I Remember Mama," "Elizabeth the Queen," "Belle of Amherst," and "The Glass Menagerie." He has led the theater to such success through the years that it is one of the ten largest professional theaters in rural America and extremely respected in regional theater circles nationwide. In 2004, Jim presented the Broadway hit musical "CATS." The Playhouse is one of only four theaters in the entire nation chosen to produce "CATS" in regional theater in the Spring of 2003. The Cumberland County playbill for the year boasts 11 wonderful plays and 12 concerts, including a beautiful version of "The Nutcracker."

By the invitation of the Rodgers and Hammerstein Organization, the Playhouse will be able to present the American premiere of a new version of "Two by Two," which was the last score composed by the great Richard Rodgers. It is also the first theater in the *world* licensed by Disney to present its classic musical, "Beauty and the Beast," independently!

The Crabtrees' gift of their time and talent to Crossville, Tennessee, is a poignant, yet powerful story. They brought Broadway theater to people who might never have had the opportunity to experience such quality entertainment. Today, Mary Crabtree is as beautiful and elegant as she was while in New York and Hollywood, and she is still a powerful leader in the theater and community. Her story continues to touch others, as does the theater.

Miller Leonard has helped to bring the Crabtrees' story to the people of Crossville, and to the leaders of Tennessee, and has been instrumental in introducing this little rural "gem" to the nation. We're thankful that she let us know the story behind this hugely successful theater—a theater that will continue to delight audiences for generations to come with world-class performances. Thank you Miller for this wonderful story that, of course, ends—"Happily Ever After!"

CALVIN LEHEW

Mr. Calvin LeHew keeps a list of three words in his office; three powerful words that have had an incredible impact on the life he has lived, the lives he has touched, and the city of Franklin, Tenn. They are the words of one of his mentors, Dr. Norman Vincent Peale: "Prayerize, Picturize, and Actualize." If you have the opportunity to meet and visit with Mr. LeHew, it will most likely be a defining moment in your life. His gentle demeanor, wealth of wisdom, optimistic outlook on life, and faith-inspired confidence have impacted thousands.

What has seemed impossible to many has become reality for Mr. LeHew, who has accomplished feats many would never dream possible. "Of course," says Mr. LeHew, "to dream it, and visualize it, makes it possible!" If you have traveled through the beautiful Natchez Trace, or visited the remarkable Factory at Franklin, you have seen the result of Calvin LeHew's visionary leadership in Franklin. It is the result of a lifetime of positive thinking, positive persistence, and positive action, coupled with an unshakable faith in God, "who makes all things possible."

Calvin LeHew was actually born in the small Tennessee town of Leipers Fork, and was, as he puts it, "backwards and insecure." Because his parents had been friends with Mr. and Mrs. Al Gore, Sr., the Gores became an important part of his life after his parents' untimely deaths. They encouraged him to further his education, and they helped him acquire positions in Washington that would eventually open many doors for him. He became a Page in the Senate in 1957 and then studied at George Washington University. Mrs. Gore encouraged him to finish his education in his home state if he wanted to be politically successful there. So, he graduated from the University of Tennessee; however, he did not pursue a career in politics.

By this time in his life, Calvin LeHew had been deeply impacted by the teachings of Dr. Norman Vincent Peale and Earl Nightingale, and he began to believe that with persistence, prayer, commitment, and a true trust in God, he would enjoy the blessings of a life filled with promise and success. He was inspired to set a lofty goal for his future, and follow it through. His goal? To be a millionaire by the time he was 35 years old. That happened, by the way, when he was only 33! Calvin and a fraternity brother opened a "discount drug store" called Freeway National Drug Store in Tallahassee, Fla., in 1963. He said, "No one could believe it, but it worked!" Many drugstores later, this Tennessee dynamo reached his monetary goal. It was only then, that Calvin LeHew realized there was something else much more important in life. He wanted to make a difference in the lives of those he loved and to his community. He and his wife then built Carter's Court, a shopping center in Franklin that soon became the seventh largest tourist attraction in Tennessee. He based this project on the wonderful, small villages of Europe, and drew some creative ideas from the famous city built by another of his mentors, Walt Disney. Mr. LeHew says that when he visited the magical streets of Disneyland, he fell in love with the hometown appeal of the place—with the sweet smell of fresh-baked pastries wafting through the air, with the familiar music that evoked memories of pleasant times, and with the cobble stone streets that reminded him of the little European villages he had visited and loved. This, he realized, would entice people. He wanted to create a place where people could visit, shop, eat, laugh, and be entertained. Those dreams soon turned into reality. When he and his wife returned from California, Mr. LeHew purchased seven old buildings in downtown Franklin. During the next seven years, he and two other businessmen formed the Downtown Franklin Merchants Association and by working with the Heritage Foundation, the City, the County and the property owners, they revitalized the downtown area. Not only did the group improve the buildings and the streetscape, they turned rents from $3 to $14 per square foot. Once this dramatic and successful project was complete, Mr. LeHew sold his seven buildings and used the earnings to purchase, restore and develop The Factory at Franklin.

Calvin and Marilyn LeHew began the colossal task of saving and restoring the former stove and bedding factory after trying to interest local business people in the idea. He even showed the property to good friend Wynonna Judd, who was looking for a place for a community center for at-risk children. He said, "Every time I showed the complex to a prospective buyer, I found something else interesting about it, and realized that I wanted to take on the project myself." Four banks turned down the "white elephant idea" before he found funding for The Factory. At that time, the land was considered more valuable without the buildings, but Calvin wanted to save those, too.

Calvin's wonderful, positive approach once again enabled him to make a dream come true. The Factory at Franklin is a complex of 14 buildings on 46 acres of land, which dates back to 1929 when it was built as a stove factory. In fact, it was home to three stove companies—Allen, Dortch, and Magic Chef—before becoming Jamison Bedding, and was eventually abandoned. Today, the historic industrial space is a bright, airy commercial venue featuring an exciting mix of retail businesses, art galleries, restaurants, and learning centers. The LeHews have set a standard for excellence with strict criteria in welcoming businesses to the Factory, and the result has been hugely successful. Where just a decade ago, downtown Franklin was a dying area, the Factory at Franklin has ushered in a revitalization and rebirth of this beautiful historic town. However, the LeHews don't want it to change too drastically. They have been vigilant in campaigning to somehow keep Franklin from becoming, "Anytown, U.S.A."

Mr. LeHew is also very proud to have been a vital part in the creation of the historic Natchez Trace. He was able to use his influence in the political field to obtain financing for the project, which has become one of the state's natural treasures.

This is just one more testament to the incredible faith and trust Calvin LeHew has in God's ability to work in and through the lives of others. He is constantly communicating his faith-filled principles to young people, hoping to empower them to reach their personal and spiritual goals. Franklin, and indeed Tennessee, have greatly benefited from the vision and hard work of Calvin LeHew, who would probably quote Dr. Peale as his advice to us all, "Throw back the shoulders, let the heart sing, let the eyes flash, let the mind be lifted up, look upward and say to yourself . . . Nothing is impossible!"

DISCOVER NASHVILLE

If you love wonderful surprises, you're in luck! The entire Middle Tennessee area holds many treasures for you to discover. From walking horse farms and Civil War battlefields to famous distilleries and hillbilly rock and roll adventures, the area is brimming with adventure and culture.

Nashville, of course, resonates throughout the entire world as Music City USA. Rich, deep Tennessee history can be found in the wonderful art galleries, historic homes and plantations, and the famous musical venues throughout the area. Very few cities in the entire world have the allure of this toe-tapping phenomenon. From its reputation as one of the South's oldest cities to its top-seed position in the music world, Nashville has been described as "an abundant blend of yesterday's history and tomorrow's legends." Maybe that's why it seems to move in a rhythm all its own…the city's creative energy captures the hearts of her visitors with a free-spirited, down-home welcome that never ends.

What's In a Name?

Throughout its history, Nashville has had many names. It has been called the Hunting Grounds, French Lick, the Bluffs, Fort Nashborough, Athens of the South, and Music City. Scientific evidence points to habitation by Paleo-Hunters thousands of years ago, and by Cherokee, Chickasaw, and Shawnee Indians later, who used the area as their hunting grounds. Frenchmen first came to "the Bluffs" as fur traders in 1710 and established a trading post near a salt lick, so it was called "French Lick." In 1778, Englishman James Robertson and his exploration group from North Carolina named the area Fort Nashborough for General Francis Nash, a Revolutionary

War hero. The name was changed to "Nashville" in 1784, and in 1843 it was named the capital of Tennessee.

You can "trace" 200 years of Tennessee history in 200 miles . . . when you travel the beautiful Avery Trace. In an effort to encourage settlers to move west and settle Tennessee, a road was cut from the south end of the Clinch Mountains in East Tennessee to French Lick (Nashville). A hunter named Peter Avery was chosen to direct the blazing of this wilderness trail. He began in 1787, laying the path along buffalo trails, which the Cherokee Indians had used as a warpath. Five forts along the Trace provided shelter and protection for travelers, with Fort Nashborough being the western-most point. A replica of the fort now stands overlooking the Cumberland River, and is open to the public for self-guided tours.

Civil War buffs know that more battles were fought in Tennessee than in any other state except Virginia, and that the war's final epic struggle, "The Last Campaign" took place right on the outskirts of Nashville. Historic sites—from Spring Hill to Franklin and into Nashville—tell the heartbreaking stories of courage, victory, and the end of the Civil War. A journey through these Civil War battlefields, known as The Antebellum Trail, enables you to feel the past come alive. It's an experience you will always remember. Every home along the trail was touched by the war, as both Confederate and Union soldiers commandeered housing and camped on the beautiful plantation lawns. There are eight sites open to the public, as well as antique shops and bed and breakfasts along the way to enhance your journey.

Education was a major concern during Nashville's early history, with classes being held on the flatboats for the children of the early explorers. Davidson Academy, which later became Cumberland University and then the University of Nashville, was established shortly after the area was settled. Also, Vanderbilt University was founded in 1873. There are now 17 colleges and universities in Nashville alone. Because Nashville was already called the "Athens of the South" because of its value as an education center, a magnificent, full-scale replica of the ancient Greek Parthenon was built for the Tennessee Centennial Exposition in 1897. Inside you'll find art galleries with ever-changing art and history exhibits, as well as a permanent collection—The Cowan Collection of American Art.

Last, but certainly not least, the nickname "Music City" was given to Nashville. A rich heritage of Anglo-American folk music came to the Bluffs with the earliest settlers. The music traveled with the flatboats and explorers to the newly settled fort, and the music resonated throughout evangelical tent meetings and gospel services. Today, the Nashville music scene is a diverse blend of rock n'roll, hip-hop, gospel, and country. Devoted fans across the country visit Nashville to explore country music's shrines, including the world-famous Country Music Hall of Fame and Museum, which spans a city block, and features displays of the pioneers of the Nashville Sound. This is the largest museum dedicated to the preservation and heritage of this distinctive type of American music. You'll discover the history of country music, see behind-the-scene films, enjoy hundreds of rare vintage photographs, experience interactive exhibits, and view a collection of rare costumes and instruments owned by celebrities. The sounds of America's rich musical heritage seem to echo throughout The Hall. You can almost hear the croonings of Willie Nelson and Hank Williams, Elvis Presley, Dolly Parton, and Loretta Lynn. And, of course a trip to Nashville would not be complete without a tour of the world-famous Ryman Auditorium. Home to the Grand Ole Opry from 1943-1974, the Ryman continues to make music history with concerts in the evening and tours by day.

History Buffs Rejoice!

The Old City Cemetery on Fourth Avenue South is one of the best places to trace the history of Nashville. Many early settlers, including James Robertson and eight Revolutionary War veterans, are buried there. It is also the final resting place for Captain William Driver—who named our flag "Old Glory," 14 mayors of Nashville; and several of the original Fisk Jubilee Singers. It was the Fisk Jubilee Singers who first brought international fame to Nashville as a music center, when they toured the United States and Europe. Its reputation as a country music center can be traced back to the 1920s when WSM radio launched the WSM Barn Dance, which later became known around the world as "The Grand Ole Opry!" Now, Nashville is home to thousands of performers, recording companies, musicians, publishers, nightclubs, and concert venues, and it holds the unchallenged title of world-wide capital of Music City.

This exciting, flamboyant, yet graceful Southern city is a

delightful melody that will live in your memory forever. It's like a catchy tune you just can't quit humming. Whether you are visiting the beautiful plantations and historic sites of her antebellum days, sashaying around the city's upscale shopping districts—many with their own names, Green Hills, Vandy, Belle Beade, Hillsboro Village—or sampling a savory selection of Southern cuisine, you will feel a true connection with this place and the lovely, talented, and very friendly people. Nashville sparkles all year as a family vacation destination. The small town charm and big city sophistication of the city offer the beauty of the past with all of the luxuries of today—first-class shopping, excellent lodging, incredible dining, and outstanding recreational entertainment. It is a city equally at home in black tie or blue jeans that invites you to "step out" and enjoy this wonderful blend of stellar performances, outstanding sporting events, and fun fairs and festivals. They all tell the story of Nashville—Music City USA!

For additional information about Nashville, contact the Nashville Area Chamber of Commerce online at www.nashvillechamber.com or call 615-743-3000. You may also contact the Nashville Convention and Visitors Bureau at 800-657-6910 or 615-259-4700, or visit www.musiccityusa.com online.

Nashville
Fairs Festivals & Fun

January
  The Upper Room Chapel & Museum Nativity Exhibit

March
  Spring Fling Flea Market

April
  Awesome April
  Nashville Film Festival
  Spring Extravaganza Flea Market
  Tin Pan South – Songwriters Festival

May
  River Stages
  Tennessee Crafts Fair

June
  CMA Music Festival
  American Artisan Festival

July
  4th of July Celebration

August
  Music City Jazz and Heritage Festival
  Fall Fest

September
  Fall Festival Flea Market
  Home Decorating and Remodeling Show

October
  Historic Brentwood Home Tour
  Tennessee's Largest Flea Market and Antique Show

November

The Upper Room Chapel & Museum Nativity Exhibit
Americana Christmas Sampler Craft, Folk Art &
    Antique Show
"A Plantation Christmas" at the Belle Meade Plantation
Festival of the Holidays at Cheekwood Botanical Gardens
    & Museum of Art
Holiday Preview Flea Market
A Country Christmas at the Gaylord Opryland Resort

December

The Upper Room Chapel & Museum Nativity Exhibit
Christmas at Belmont at the Belmont Mansion
A Country Christmas at the Gaylord Opryland Resort
Trees of Christmas at Cheekwood Botanical Gardens
    & Museum of Art
"A Plantation Christmas" at the Belle Meade Plantation
Music City Bowl

Antiques, Art & Furniture

Bradford's

For those who love fine home furnishings and European antiques, Bradford's, 4100 Hillsboro Rd., is a must-see. For more than 100 years, Bradford's has furnished Nashville's finest homes. There are very few full-line, full-service home furnishing stores left in the country, but Bradford's has maintained its dedication to providing customers with the best of interior design—from floor to ceiling and everything in between.

Antiques are hand-picked in Europe, specifically for the Southern market, and Bradford's Oriental Rug Gallery has won national acclaim for outstanding selection and service. Also, Bradford's fabric library is one of the largest and most complete in the South. Open Monday-Friday 9 am-5:30 pm and Saturday 10 am-5:30 pm. For more information, call 615-297-3541.

The Artful Dog

"an awesome art & garden gallery"

This is one art and garden gallery that has literally "gone to the dogs." Sherri Alper's very unique shop is charming, inspiring, and doggone fun! The Artful Dog is located in an old cottage at 2828 Dogwood, in the Berry Hill Shopping District of Nashville. This wonderful shop consists of an amazing collection of fun, folk and functional art, featuring but not limited to woman's and man's best friend.

Sherri started the business in 2001 with a different name, location, and focus, carrying mostly garden antiques and vintage architectural pieces. But thanks to Rugby, her laid-back Jack Russell Terrier shop dog and "spokesman," and some unusual tin replicas of him by a local artist, she slowly started moving the shop in a new direction. She relocated, changed the name to The Artful Dog, and then the fun began. First, she searched for aspiring or established artists with a whimsical style. Then she began acquiring their art, in all mediums from mosaics to paintings on tin to ironwork. Today, animal art, garden art, and folk art sit amongst and atop vintage architectural pieces, small antiques, and other finds. She says the shop is still "a work of art in progress" but successfully evolving into a great source for original art, one-of-a-kind gifts, and unique décor for the home, garden, and dog lover's domain.

Sherri has recently acquired another laid-back Jack Russell Terrier, Rascal. She has also expanded the shop to include "The Artful Dig," a garage shop for artists and "artists" and "The Jack Russell Terror Yard" which you'll just have to see! The Artful Dog is usually open seven days a week, unless Sherri is on a buying trip, or selling at a show or benefit. Call 615-269-6920 or visit www.artfuldog.com for more information and directions.

Re Creations

"The eclectic and unique is truly our niche," say Owners Tim Causey and Richard Epperson when describing their home design boutique, ReCreations. Together, Tim and Richard have pooled their energies, resources and talents together in an effort to provide customers with the ultimate in home accessories, floral designs, antiques and fine furniture. They are never satisfied with the ordinary and are always searching for new and different products. So prepare to be amazed!

ReCreations offers a breathtaking collection of treasures from the four corners of the world. The ambiance of the 12,000 square foot store truly makes shopping a pleasure. Once you enter, you will find yourself captivated by the great selection of merchandise and its affordability. Every nook and cranny of the store is filled with everything from crocodile leather armchairs and mirrored vanity stools to vases of all sizes, filled with long Canadian pheasant feathers, flanking granite-top vanities. The reason for this is simple—an amazing interior makes your home amazing, and that is their goal!

"We're in the specialty business," says Tim, "We're kind of a one-stop shop. We're able to do a little bit of everything for the customer." Both Tim and Richard realize what customers want as far as style, selection, quality and service and they won't settle for giving you second best. They've discovered that attention to detail is the key to being successful, so you'll appreciate the superb customer service and expert advice that they provide. ReCreations also offers home consultations so that you can enjoy that special treatment and style in your own home. Don't miss the wonderful annual Christmas Open House, the first full weekend of October.

Stop by and see for yourself—you won't be disappointed! ReCreations, 4319 Sidco Dr. in Nashville, is open daily 10 am-7 pm. For more information, call 615-834-0055. *(Color photo featured in front section of book.)*

Chancery Lane Antiques

Chancery Lane Antiques, 5133 Harding Rd. in Nashville, is the result of Doris Matthews Lebo's lifetime interest in antique silver. In fact, she purchased her first pair of silver salt dishes when she was just 14 years old. Her interest grew even more while traveling abroad and as the guest of a local silver dealer. Her parents, Russell and Corneila Speights, started the silver collection at Cheekwood Museum during the early 1960s, and Doris began adding to her growing collection. You'll find more than 3,500 items at Chancery Lane Antiques includ-

ing: tea-sets; serving trays; trophy cups; hand mirrors; christening sets; card cases; perfume bottles; and tortoiseshell boxes. Hours are Monday-Friday 11 am-5 pm and Saturday 11 am-4 pm. Call 615-354-0400 or visit www.chancerylane.com.

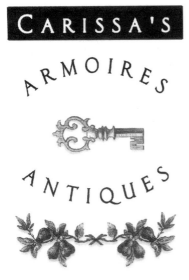

CARISSA'S ARMOIRES ANTIQUES

One visit to Carissa's Armoires & Antiques and you'll immediately know this is not a typical antique store. More than 5,000 square feet of shopping space accommodates unique accessories, armoires, chests, tables, chairs, and much, much more! Located in the heart of historic Hillsboro Village in Nashville, at 1801 21st Ave. S., you will find an ever-changing, always extraordinary assortment of treasures. Open Monday-Saturday 10 am-6 pm. For more information, visit www.carissasarmoires.com or call 615-292-6994.

When Betty Lawhon launched her venture into the antique business, she paved the way for other entrepreneurs. Green Hills Antique Mall at 4108 Hillsboro Rd. in Nashville features more than 70 antique dealers with a wide range of items from silver to leather-bound books. A grand stairway leads to the shops and vignettes that are filled with many extraordinary antiques and collectibles. The mall is open Monday-Saturday 10 am-5:30 pm. For more information, call 615-383-9851 or 615-383-3893.

Gilchrist Gilchrist

Whimsical. Vintage Chic. These are the words that best describe Gilchrist Gilchrist. Overflowing with vintage furniture and accessories, this magical cottage will fill you with child-like excitement. You'll wander through the beautiful displays and feel like you've entered your own personal wonderland.

Gilchrist Gilchrist is the realized dream of owner Genia Gilchrist, and she definitely takes pride in it. Filled with all the things she's sure you'll love—vintage handbags, fragrant candles, and other yummy whimsies—Genia creates a feminine retreat for the girly girl in all of us. Interior stylists are available upon request.

Gilchrist Gilchrist, 2823 Bransford Ave. in Nashville, is open Monday-Saturday 10 am-5 pm. Call 615-385-2122.

For more than 30 years, Pembroke Antiques has specialized in handpicked, beautiful English and French Country furniture. Visit the friendly staff and owner Laura Doolittle while you shop for special gifts or perfect home furnishings. With plenty of parking, the shop is located at 6610 Hwy. 100 in Nashville. Hours are Monday-Saturday 10 am-5 pm. Call 615-353-0889.

Berenice Denton
Estate Sales & Appraisals
B. Denton's Cottage

Visit Berenice Denton's Estate Sales & Appraisals and B. Denton's Cottage, which is filled with antiques, art, furniture, jewelry, and consignment items, 2209-C Bandywood Dr. in Nashville. Open Monday-Friday 10 am-5 pm and Saturday until 4 pm. Call 615-292-5765 or visit www.BereniceDenton.com.

Attractions, Entertainment & Museums

CENTER FOR THE VISUAL ARTS

Located in Nashville's historic former main post office at 919 Broadway, the Frist Center for the Visual Arts is an art exhibition center dedicated to presenting the finest visual art from local, regional, national, and international sources in a program of ever-changing exhibitions. Its mission is not only to offer art to view, but also to encourage visitors to connect with the art. The gallery has more than 20,000-square-feet of exhibition space and includes a landscaped courtyard; an education gallery; studio/classrooms; a state-of-the-art media resource center; a café; a retail store; and a 250-seat auditorium. The Frist Center offers ways for visitors to interact with art including many hands-on opportunities. In fact, each week hundreds of visitors participate in art activities in ArtQuest, the Frist Center's state-of-the-art interactive gallery. A visit to the Frist Center Gift Shop offers an eclectic assortment of merchandise from around the world, from Baltic Amber jewelry and decorative art glass to art books and collectable posters. Plan to enjoy lunch afterwards in the Frist Center Café, which opens onto the beautifully-landscaped Turner Courtyard.

The Center was named for Dr. Thomas F. Frist, Jr., whose family's philanthropic support was responsible for the Frist Center's creation. Dr. Frist serves as Chairman of the Board of Trustees.

The Center is open to the public Monday-Saturday 10 am to 5:30 pm, Thursday until 8 pm and Sunday 1-5 pm. Admission is free for children 18 and younger. For information call 615-244-3340 or visit www.fristcenter.org online.

Located only minutes from downtown, the Nashville Zoo offers more than just a simple "trip to the zoo." Hyacinth macaw, Manchurian Cranes, and vocal Gibbons greet visitors in the new Entry Village. Meerkats, cheetah, ostrich, zebra, tigers, elephants, cougars, otters and others can be seen on the animal trail. "Critter Encounters" lets young ones get up close and personal to goats, sheep and camels. And, this is just a sample of the wild and wonderful things you'll experience at Nashville's expanding Zoo. Located at 3777 Nolensville Rd., land for the present site was donated by sisters Margaret and Elise Croft, who owned the Grassmere property. Following their deaths in 1985, the Cumberland Science Museum began development of the 200-acre property, which opened as the Grassmere Wildlife Park. Seven years later, the original Nashville Zoo, which was located in Joelton, moved to the Grassmere property, and growth has exceeded the city's wildest expectations. The new convenient location and increased acreage has allowed the zoo to offer many new community events and children's activities such as the Jungle Gym playground. It's the largest community-built playground in the United States, featuring more than 66,000 square feet of slides, swings, and exploration structures. Don't miss the Unseen New World, an outstanding indoor exhibit space with more than 200 species of reptiles, fish, insects, and amphibians! Also, make time to experience the Historic Home and Working Farm to see what life was like in the 19th century. The Nashville Zoo is open daily 9 am-4 pm (November-March) and until 6 pm (April-October). Call 615-833-1534 or visit www.nashvillezoo.org online.

TOURS & CASINO DEPOT

Explore the wonderful attractions of Nashville through one of the most respected tour companies in the country. Gray Line Tours, 2416 Music Valley Dr., was started and operated by brothers Chris and Dennis Levering, who were both raised in Nashville. They have owned the company for more than 30 years and currently own the largest privately-owned motorcoach company in Tennessee.

Gray Line offers 12 daily tours highlighting the very best of Nashville. The most popular "Discover Nashville Tour" is an all-inclusive 3½ hour adventure through downtown Nashville, Fort Nashborough, the State Capital, the Parthenon, Vanderbilt University, and Music Row. You'll see the Ryman Auditorium—the Mother Church of Country Music—and tour the incredible Country Music Hall of Fame.

The "Home of the Stars" tour is so much fun, and a "must" for all country music lovers! This tour gives fans a glimpse of the beautiful homes of superstars such as Alan Jackson, Vince Gill and Amy Grant, Ronnie Milsap, Dolly Parton, Bryan White, Martina McBride, Ronnie Dunn and Kix Brooks, Trisha Yearwood, Lori Ann Crook, and Little Jimmy Dickens.

If you can plan a dinner tour, the General Jackson Dinner Cruise is absolutely wonderful. You will enjoy a seated 3-course dinner and exciting stage show as you cruise the Cumberland River in a four-deck paddle wheeler reminiscent of bygone days.

Gray Line Tours has also partnered with Casino Depot to offer exciting trips to Nashville's closest gaming destinations. Same day trips to Harrah's and Casino Aztar are only two hours away. Overnight and day trips to Tunica, the South's largest gaming destination, are also available. Open 8 am-6 pm daily. For more information, visit online www.graylinenashville.com or www.casinodepot.net, or call 800-251-1864 or 615-883-5555.

A trip to Nashville is not complete without a visit to one of its most famous treasures—the Ryman Auditorium. This National Historic Landmark first opened its doors at 116 Fifth Ave. N. in 1892 as The Union Gospel Tabernacle—a vision of Captain Thomas G. Ryman. It was renamed the Ryman Auditorium in 1904 upon his death. When Captain Ryman was converted by a Southern evangelist in 1885, he decided to build a tabernacle for the city's revivals. Through the years, the tabernacle hosted revivals, lectures, ballets, operas, musical and theater performances, political debates, boxing matches, and even livestock sales. In the 1930s, the Ryman was called the "Carnegie Hall of the South." With the coming of the Grand Ole Opry show in 1943, the Ryman found its identity as "The Mother Church of Country Music," hosting famous performers such as Cowboy Copas, Chet Atkins, Grandpa Jones, Hank Williams Sr., Patsy Cline and Johnny Cash. When the Opry left the Ryman in 1974, the auditorium remained vacant for many years. An $8.5 million renovation was completed in 1994, which revived this performance hall whose acoustics surpass even Carnegie Hall, and are second only to the Mormon Tabernacle. We loved the wonderful bronze tribute to legendary performers— Minnie Pearl and Roy Acuff. Today, the beautiful Ryman Auditorium has once again stepped to "center stage" as a national showplace and premier performance hall. In early 2004, the Ryman was named America's "Theatre of the Year" at the Pollstar Concert Industry Awards in Hollywood. The visual displays tell the stories of its rich history, and the sounds of rock, bluegrass, gospel, pop, country, and classical music fill the air. It is open to the public daily 9 am-4 pm. Times for evening shows vary. Backstage tours are now available. Call 615-458-8700 or visit www.ryman.com.

Bed & Breakfasts

THE TIMOTHY DEMONBREUN HOUSE

For comfortable accommodations and private dining at its finest, folks return again and again to Nashville's premiere Bed & Breakfast, The Timothy Demonbreun House located just one mile south of downtown in a lovely historic district at 746 Benton Ave. Throughout the year The House hosts Southern-style outdoor weddings, rehearsal dinners, private dining, cocktail parties, luaus, luncheons and corporate retreats on its spacious front lawn and in its elegant front foyer. Listed on the National Registry of Historic Places, this incredible mansion has been completely restored inside and out, and contains everything from a third-floor billiard/poker room and antique wine cellar to a heated swimming pool and spa.

Call owner Richard Demonbreun at 615-383-0426 for reservations. You are invited to drop by for a tour of this incredible 22-room showcase or visit www.tdhouse.com online.

Davis·Kidd
Booksellers

Before the era of brand-name chain bookstores, two social workers took a chance on a lifelong dream. Friends Karen Davis and Thelma Kidd dreamt of a place where they could combine their love of books and a cozy place for people to relax. They also thought it would be nice to offer coffee and big comfy chairs. They were forward thinkers. Despite predictions of failure, Davis-Kidd Booksellers successfully opened in 1980 as one of the first and most unique bookstore/coffee shops in Nashville.

Today, Davis-Kidd Booksellers, 4007 Hillsboro Rd. in Nashville, flourishes in a building across the street from its original location. The move not only allowed the bookstore to grow in size, but also in content. The two-story building houses a plethora of books ranging across every genre and reading level. Comfy chairs and couches are spread around the store for their visitors' enjoyment and, on the second level, the Bronte bistro provides sandwiches and pizza for hungry lunchers and anything from pasta to quesadillas for later diners.

Davis-Kidd Booksellers continues to create unique ideas that draw readers back time and time again, making it a favorite hangout for locals. Whether it's a lecture, a storyteller time or a book signing, Davis-Kidd stays full of excitement and activities for all ages.

Hours are Monday-Saturday 9 am-10 pm and Sunday 10 am-7 pm, stop by! For more information, call 615-385-2645 or visit www.daviskidd.com online.

JAMIE, INC.

The magnificent wood doors with the handsome brass handles hint of the elegance you'll find inside Jamie, Inc., 4317 Harding Rd. This very up-scale fashion boutique and "beauty lab" offers the ultimate in one-stop shopping for the discriminating women of Nashville. Located in the beautiful residential area called Belle Meade, Jamie, Inc. has been a mainstay for many years as "the place" to find the finest designer and contemporary clothing, fine jewelry and accessories. From  Gucci handbags and shoes to beautiful gemstone jewelry, you'll find something absolutely wonderful! The second floor of Jamie, Inc. contains a hair salon called Elements, where customers can take advantage of the professional beauty lab staff for manicures, pedicures, facials, or the latest cosmetic advice. The store is open Monday-Friday 10 am-5:30 pm and until 5 pm on Saturday. Call 615-292-4188.

REBECKA VAUGHAN LINGERIE

After a career in nursing, Rebecka Vaughan decided to open a shop "just for women"—a lingerie shop where she could help women find the perfect lingerie no matter their circumstances or size. Doctors often refer their patients to Rebecka for breast prosthesis. Rebecka Vaughan Lingerie at 4004 Hillsboro Rd. has been in this same location for more than 25 years and has become known as "the foundation center" of Nashville and surrounding towns. Rebecka carries many styles of bras from 30AA-56J. Whether you are looking for bras; panties; girdles; corsets; nightgowns; or robes; you will love the selection. Brides-to-be will find fabulous honeymoon attire! The friendly, helpful staff is discreet and accommodating. The shop is open Monday-Saturday 9:30 am- 5:30 pm. Call 615-269-4413.

PROP-R-FIT SHOES

Are your dogs barking? Then go see Parveen Sood at Prop-R-Fit Shoes, 3706 Hillsboro Rd. in Nashville. After selling shoes for many years, Parveen saw that people needed shoes that were measured to properly fit their feet. She and her husband Bhupinder provide prescription and thermally-molded footwear for men and women. Besides the brands she carries such as Birkenstock, Ecco, Mephisto, and New Balance, there is an on-site laboratory area staffed by technicians who take molds of the feet for custom-made shoes. Prop-R-Fit Shoes hours are Monday-Friday 10 am-6 pm and Saturday until 5 pm. Call 615-292-1934 or visit www.properfitshoes.com online.

We love the name of this store, *and* everything in it! Ken and Julie Lutz told us that the word "Serendipity" means, "to find a treasure in an unexpected place." That certainly is the case here. You'll find unique clothing at affordable prices; wonderful sterling jewelry; and gorgeous gift items. Two of the most exciting items in the store are the unique line of washable linen clothing from New York called "Flax," and an imported line found in Prague, Czechoslovakia, called Morning Star. Other treasures include: great handbags; scarves; and belts; picture frames; vases; and handmade soaps. You will love this cute, funky, cool store located at 2301 12th Ave. S. in Nashville, *and* the fact that you have found "serendipity!" It is open Monday-Saturday 10 am-7 pm. Call 615-279-5570.

Zelda

Don't miss Zelda! Featured in both *Victoria* and *Shopping Savvy* magazines, this fascinating shop brims with everything — casual clothing, dressy outfits, nontraditional bridal, unique accessories, antique jewelry, and even loose gemstones and handmade jewelry. Owner Marsha Mason Hunt shops worldwide to fill this unusual boutique and even designs some items herself. And, there's no telling who you might see at Zelda — many local music personalities are also customers! Visit Zelda at 5133 Harding Rd. in Nashville (615-356-2430) until the relocation in August 2004. Then you'll find Zelda at 4100 Hillsboro Circle (615-292-8045) Monday through Saturday 10:30 am-5 pm.

THE FRENCH SHOPPE
LADIES' APPAREL

With four locations throughout the Nashville area, you'll have every opportunity to enjoy all of the beautiful clothing and accessories from The French Shoppe. Ohh la la! You'll love this store. Wardrobe consultation is one of the special services that has made this beautiful upscale fashion boutique a local favorite. You'll find classic business attire, exciting evening dresses, fun casual wear, and wonderful jewelry and accessories to complete every ensemble. The store at 2817 West End Ave. is open Monday-Friday 10 am-6 pm and Saturday until 5 pm. For more information and for other locations, call 615-327-8712.

JENSEN TRAVELWEAR by JACQUELINE

Are you a busy woman with little time to worry about clothes that wrinkle or outfits that travel poorly? If so, you'll want to visit Jensen Travelwear by Jacqueline at www.jensentravelwear.com online. Since 1999, this company has created comfortable, stylish clothing for women on the go. For more information, store locations, and to request a catalog, call 888-821-0979.

TIBA

DE NUHAD KHOURY

Spa • Parfumerie • Accessories • Gifts

As you unwind at Tiba, Nashville's No. 1 Day Spa, take time to peruse the unparalleled selection of fine accessories, jewelry, perfumes, cosmetics and gifts from around the world. You'll find the dazzling designer collections of John Hardy; Patricia Von Musulin; Rigoberto; and Cassandra of Italy; as well as elegant and distinctive boudoir/bath accessories; ornate and whimsical hair accessories; and even sophisticated hats from Milan, New York, and Paris.

Select from the exclusive skincare offerings of Orlane, LaPrairie, Cellcosmet, and Ingrid Millet. Or, dabble in the decadence of French perfumes. Discover what Tiba already knows—you deserve the best.

Stop by Tiba, located at 2126 Abbott Martin Rd., #132 in The Mall at Green Hills, Monday-Friday 10 am-9 pm, Saturday until 8 pm and Sunday 1-6 pm. Call 615-269-5121, 800-964-6868, or visit www.tibaspa.com online. *(Color photo featured in front section of book.)*

You're Invited!

gifts & paper

Belle Meade Galleria

Building relationships with clients that will last a lifetime is what owner Kendall Archdeacon of You're Invited is committed to doing. Voted Nashville Retail Business Woman Owner of the Year in 2002, Kendall provides outstanding customer service and a wide range of gift and stationery products that will fit any occasion.

When you're planning a special event—a wedding, christening, bar mitzvah or anything else—you need to find invitations and gifts that reflect your personal style and taste. From the fun and fancy-free to the elegant and engraved, You're Invited offers invitations and gifts that are as distinctive as you are.

For the bride-to-be, You're Invited provides an extensive gift registry that is known throughout the area. You'll find a vast selection of hand-painted pottery by Vicki Carroll, Present Tense and Gail Pittman. Or come find the perfect bridesmaid and groomsman gifts. And—you'll be pleasantly pleased to know monogramming services are available as well.

You're Invited also carries a variety of other items like charming holiday cards, magnificent metal art trays, beautiful baby gifts, terrific teacher appreciation gifts, and much more. You'll also love the variety of unique purses—we found it difficult to choose just one!

You're Invited, 5133 Harding Pike, in Nashville's Belle Meade Galleria, is open 10 am-6 pm Monday-Friday and Saturday from 10 am-4 pm. Just look for the store's inviting pink awnings; they're a prelude to the treasures you'll find inside. For more information, call 615-353-5520 or 866-468-4833.

As beautiful as its name, this garden and gift boutique, 2800 Bransford Ave. in Nashville, is the culmination of talents between Jason White and Nancy Robison. Eden offers a diverse array of gifts, garden art, birdhouses, tools, and more! This little "Eden" is filled with seasonal greens; annuals and perennials; mums and pansies; and Christmas trees, wreaths, and garland. Open Monday-Saturday 10 am-5 pm. Call 615-383-0038 for extended seasonal hours or visit www.edengardenstore.com.

Happiness Place

Looking for the perfect gift? Since 1984, Owner Judy Carroll has offered customers beautiful gift and home décor items. As you shop, you'll be inspired by Happiness Place's imaginative flair—something Judy has been able to create thanks to her artistic upbringing—her father was an accomplished musician and her mother a very creative florist. Happiness Place, 2144 Bandywood Dr. in Nahville, is open Monday-Friday, 10 am-5 pm and Saturday 10 am-4 pm. Call 615-383-1034.

"I'm not offended by all the dumb blonde jokes because I know I'm not dumb . . . and I'm also not blonde."

— Dolly Parton

GAYLORD OPRYLAND™

RESORT & CONVENTION CENTER

It is called the "Crown Jewel" of the Gaylord Hotel family—a showcase resort that lavishes guests with genuine Southern delights and hospitality. As soon as you walk through the front doors of Nashville's Gaylord Opryland Resort & Convention Center, you will know why the tagline is "Everything in One Place. So You Can Have It All." With 2,881 guestrooms; 600,000 square feet of meeting space; five ballrooms; nine acres of lush gardens soaring under glass rooftops; cascading waterfalls; an indoor river with flatboat cruises; six restaurants; five lounges; four eateries; a state-of-the-art video games arcade; a cyber café; a fitness center; and two pools, Gaylord Opryland truly offers everything under one incredible roof. Beyond the physical amenities, guests experience the ambience of true Southern hospitality from the friendly staff. They call them "STARS"—Smiles, Teamwork, Attitude, Respect, and Service with a passion. You'll get it all at this incredibly beautiful resort.

Although Gaylord Opryland has been recognized as being the "best in the business," it has never been content to rest on past success. The Opryland Pavilion opened June 2004,

with 37,000 square feet of versatile space for banquets, concerts, or business exhibitions. Scheduled to open summer of 2005 is the posh spa "Relache," which will compliment the epic beauty of the property's world-famous atriums. Although the name is a French derivative of a word meaning "relax," the ambience will be true Southern hospitality! The hotel is located at 2800 Opryland Dr. For reservations, call toll-free 888-976-2000, or visit www.gaylordhotels.com online. Be sure to ask about the incredible holiday events. *(Featured on the front cover.)*

Featuring the Richardsonian Romanesque architecture of the 1800s, Union Station–A Wyndham Historic Hotel stands as an elegant reminder of its romantic past. This amazing hotel was built as a train station in 1896, opened in 1900, and was transformed into the masterpiece it is today in 1986. The original 65-foot barrel vaulted ceiling is made of exquisite stained glass, and the lobby is filled with original gold leaf mirrors. Choose from 125 luxurious guestrooms—historic yet modern. From the pillow-top mattresses and down comforters to the fuzzy slippers and cozy bathrobe provided, you will feel very pampered. There is also 12,000-square-feet available for private conferences or business seminars. The Union Station, 1001 Broadway in Nashville, is also a favorite place for weddings. Be sure to visit www.wyndham.com for information or reservations, or call 615-726-1001.

THE HERMITAGE HOTEL

You'll feel pampered the minute you check into The Hermitage Hotel, with its warm and friendly service and the finest luxury guest rooms and suites around. Plan to dine in one of its fine restaurants and visit the gift shop for sundries, unique gifts, or cappuccino.

The Hermitage, built in 1910, boasts a rich history, having been graced with some of the nation's most prominent figures—from presidents to war heroes—a place where "Meet me at The Hermitage" remained a popular slogan throughout the early part of the 20th century.

A member of Preferred Hotels & Resorts Worldwide, this five Diamond historic luxury hotel hosts some of the grandest events in Nashville. For more information, stop by at 231 Sixth Ave. N. or visit www.thehermitagehotel.com online. To learn more, call 888-888-9414 or 615-244-3121.

VANDERBILT

Courtyard Marriott at 1901 West End Ave. in Nashville is not only a great place to stay, it's also an award-winning location—recognizing General Manager Bill Ghumm and Operations Manager Adrienne Griffin with a Tennessee Hotel & Lodging Association Honor. This hotel opened in 1995 minus the brand-recognized gazebo that makes a Courtyard by Marriott

hotel complete, so the staff placed a picture of a gazebo in the lobby. In 1999, the demand for rooms at this location justified an addition. Four years after its opening, this location proudly added a cozy gazebo flower garden, making them "officially" a Courtyard by Marriott. The gazebo picture remains in the lobby as a reminder for all who know the tale! Call 800-245-1959, 615-327-9900 or visit www.courtyard.com/bnawe online.

Bedroom Elegance/Betty Jan Interiors brings true meaning to the word 'elegance.' You'll see why when you visit 2146 Bandywood Dr. in Nashville. Betty Jan, owner and designer, has provided elegant décor to homes and businesses since 1969.

You'll find beautiful lamps, art, gifts, and floral, as well as custom-designed bedding, upholstered headboards, pillows, tabletops and window treatments in stock—there are hundreds of patterns to choose from, ready to take home or to ship.

At the urging of friends and clients in Hendersonville, a second shop opened fall 2003. A visit to 387-A W. Main St. is a must! Each shop is delightful! Watch for the opening of a third store in the Spring of 2005. You will enjoy shopping at Bedroom Elegance—we did! The Nashville shop is open Monday-Friday 10 am-5 pm and Saturday until 4 pm. The Hendersonville shop is open Thursday-Saturday 8 am-5 pm. Call 615-292-0106.

BELLA LINEA®

The name means "beautiful linens" in Italian. That is an understatement, because the incredible linens and decorative accessories at Bella Linea are absolutely the most elegant and luxurious you will find anywhere. Nashvillian Linda Berry, who noticed a great interest in linens made from Egyptian cotton, founded Bella Linea in 1987. She saw that people who had traveled or lived abroad were seeking linens that would last a lifetime, both in style and quality. From the time she opened her first Bella Linea, Linda has endeavored to bring the quality and charm of fine European linens to America. In fact, Bella Linea is considered by the linens industry to be among the top 10 of this kind in the United States.

Linda has two very beautiful stores, one in Nashville at 6031 Hwy. 100 (just a few blocks from BelleMeade, the queen of antebellum plantations) and one in Franklin at 335 Main St. (just off the historic town square).

The designers at Bella Linea can help you create a private sanctuary filled with comfort and elegance. There are duvets, sheets, shams, bed skirts, and bedcovers, available in every color and pattern imaginable. You can choose a fine Italian damask woven from a 300-thread count Egyptian cotton, or crib sheets and duvets for your nursery. Indulge yourself in fluffy goose down comforters, pillows, or featherbeds, or gorgeous matelasse bedcovers. You'll also find a variety of accents to define your special rooms, such as handmade iron beds, French antiques, tables, lamps and chairs.

Whether you are looking for an exceptional gift for a bride or newborn, or just treating yourself for a change, Bella Linea is the store for you. Hours are Monday through Saturday 10 am-6 pm. Call 615-352-4041 in Nashville or 615-627-1884 in Franklin or visit www.bellalinea.com online.

Matchmaker! Matchmaker! A former high school teacher now in business for 28 years, Ro Buxbaum has the knowledge and experience to find that right rug or tapestry. Ro says, "I search internationally for the oriental rug or tapestry that reflects the client's needs." You'll find the largest selection of old and antique rugs in Nashville and of period European tapestries in the Southeast. Visit 6021 Hwy. 100 in the Westgate Center, Monday-Saturday 10 am-5 pm. Call 615-352-9055.

Tennessee Memories is a specialty gift shop located in the Green Hills shopping area of Nashville, 2182 Bandywood Dr. The store carries lines of pottery made in Tennessee, wood gifts, Tennessee pewter and other products made in the wonderful state of Tennessee. And, the pantry is filled with Tennessee food products, just perfect for filling custom-made gift baskets. Hours are Monday-Saturday 10 am-5:30 pm and Sundays 1-5 pm in December. Visit www.tennesseememories.com, call 615-298-3253 or fax 615-298-3294.

Maitland's

A Permanent Botanical Shoppe

The incredible permanent botanicals and arrangements at Maitland's, 2205 Bandywood Dr. in Nashville, are the finest around. Owner/horticulturist Candy Maitland takes great care that every item she sells is "botanically correct." You'll find permanent trees, plants, and flowers, as well as dried, freeze-dried, and preserved materials. Open Monday-Friday 10 am-5:30 pm and Saturday until 3 pm. Call 615-385-3434 or visit www.maitlandsbotanicals.com.

Jewelry

Cindi Earl

The first thing you will notice about this beautiful fine jewelry store is the open and light atmosphere. An entire wall of windows allows natural light to flood the space. This dispels the museum "look but don't touch" atmosphere, which suits owner Cindi Earle to a "T." Cindi has been in Tennessee for more than 20 years, but this native Texan still loves the "wide open spaces." Her new location at 5101 Harding Rd. in Nashville is just the kind of "wide open space" she fancies.

Cindi's exciting new store features fashion-forward fine jewelry. The designer lines include Alex Sepkus, Chad Allison, Gregg Ruth, and Erica Courtney. You'll also find traditional diamond bands, bridal mountings, and fun affordable jewelry. "We present the best to our community in a way that is exclusive but does not exclude," Cindi shares. The store hours are Monday-Saturday 10 am-5:30 pm. Call 615-353-1823.

"A Bead for Every Need," is The Beaded Bungalow's motto. You'll find a variety of European glass beads from seed beads to large Venetian, faceted semi-precious gemstones, fresh water pearls and more. Owners Phil and Victoria Lovett travel far and wide to find one-of-a-kind pieces, hand-picked for their unique qualities. For the experienced designer, you'll love the unique findings available. And for the beginner, you'll find on-staff designers ready to help you create beautiful designs. If you want to learn how to create beaded accessories, Christmas ornaments or advanced off-loom beadwork, classes are available. "Our customers want to be proud of their creations," says Victoria, "and we want to be proud of what we offer them." The Beaded Bungalow, 2816 Bransford Ave., in the quaint Berry Hill area of Nashville, is open 10 am-7 pm on Monday, 10 am-6 pm Tuesday-Friday, and Saturday 10 am-5 pm. Call 615-298-5030.

"I never worry about diets.
The only carrots that interest me
are the number you get in a diamond."

– Mae West

BERNINA®

SEWING CENTER

BERNINA · JANOME · PFAFF

Barbara Hooper says, "We are a family-owned-and-operated small business, and plan to remain so." She, husband Don, and daughter Daphne work together in making the Bernina-Janome-Pfaff Sewing Center a wonderfully successful Nashville business. Because the Sewing Center has remained small, it is able to offer its faithful customers outstanding personal service. Whether you need repair on a machine, instructions on an application, or just a congratulatory hug for a sewing triumph, Barbara and clan have got you covered.

You'll find the most technologically advanced sewing machines from Bernina, Janome and Pfaff. It's a seamstress' dream come true! The Hoopers know that buying a good machine today is quite an investment and an important decision. They also know that you'll be able to receive the attention and information you need at their center. Buying from an authorized dealer such as this center, ensures that you will receive instruction for using the machine, as well as service by certified technicians if needed. Most of these premiere machines are computerized, with mini monitors and special monogramming features.

Barbara, Don, and Daphne welcome both accomplished seamstresses and beginning enthusiasts to come in for a demonstration or to sign up for a sewing or embroidery class. They have built a relationship over the years with their many faithful customers, which is why long-time customers feel comfortable stopping in for sewing advice. There is always something new and exciting to discover here, and the owners are extremely knowledgeable and friendly. The Center, located inside Textile Fabric at 2717 Franklin Pike in Nashville, is open Monday through Saturday 10 am-5:30 pm. For more information, call 615-269-9081.

METAMORPHOSIS

Donna Benning is "living her dream," in this most wonderful needlework and stitchery store at 2176 Bandywood Dr. in Nashville. Metamorphosis is a truly happy place, filled with stitchery lovers of all ages working together, laughing, and sharing ideas—just what Donna envisioned for her unique store. Customers will find an extensive selection of beadwork, blackwork, counted cross and needlepoint, hardanger, pulled and drawn work, reproduction samplers, silk ribbon embroidery, tatting, thread crochet, whitework, and many other combinations of linen stitches. The

store is open Tuesday-Saturday 10 am-5 pm. For more information, visit www.metamorphosisinc.com online or call 615-292-4228. Both novice and expert stitchers will love this store. It's quite an experience!

angel hair

✳ ✳

yarn co.

This is not, as they say, "your grandmother's yarn shop!" In fact, Angel Hair Yarn Co., 4117 Hillsboro Pike #102 in Nashville, is owned by two young, energetic women—Pam Butler and Andrea Jones. It seems that recently "everyone" is learning to "knit one, purl two." And, Andrea and Pam are excited to offer the finest yarns as well as needles, accessories and patterns. Angel Hair carries the best selection of luxury fibers in the mid-state, and employs an extremely knowledgeable staff to help make your selections. It's a friendly, comfortable place to be; whether you are taking one of their classes; selecting yarn for a new project; or just enjoying the company and conversation of fellow knitters. Angel Hair Yarn Co. is open Monday 10 am-8 pm and Tuesday-Saturday 10 am-6 pm. But, April-July 4th, open Saturday 10 am-3 pm. To learn more, visit www.angelhairyarn.com or call 615-269-8833.

The Food Company is one of Nashville's favorite little eateries, and definitely the place for pick-up or party food. Conveniently located in Green Hills, you will enjoy the relaxed atmosphere and delicious informal food. You'll love the made from scratch Oven Roasted Pulled Turkey Sandwiches, Citrus Mint Tea Punch and the Chunky Tomato Basil Soup—they sell 90 gallons a week! Everything is wonderful! The famous Greenhouse Bar on the property is literally a bar constructed of tree trunks housed in a real greenhouse—plants and all. It is the perfect place to enjoy a cocktail, or host a private party. The Food Company, 2211 Bandywood Dr., can take care of all of your catering needs, and is open Monday-Friday 10 am-9 pm, Saturday until 5 pm and Sunday 11 am-5 pm. For more information, contact Jackie Daniel at 615-385-4311.

Sperry's Restaurant has been a favorite haunt for locals since 1974 and is a second-generation establishment located at 5109 Harding Rd. in the affluent Belle Meade neighborhood of Nashville. The warm, comfortable "Old-English" décor is complimented by three stone fireplaces, and tabletops made from World War II Liberty ship hatch covers. The menu features a wide variety of USDA Choice grain-fed beef, fresh seafood, and Nashville's first and finest salad bar. Sperry's has received the *Wine Spectator's* "Award of Excellence." The lounge is open 5-11 pm; dinner service begins at 5:30 pm. Call 615-353-0809 or visit www.sperrys.com for more information.

SoBro Grill is located within the Country Music Hall of Fame and Museum at 222 Fifth Ave. S. — SOuth of BROadway. Utilizing locally-grown produce and made-from-scratch recipes, the chef offers up a contemporary spin on the "greatest hits" of Southern cuisine—fresh salads, piled-high sandwiches and Southern specialties. Serving lunch from 11 am-2:30 pm during museum visiting days and closed on Sundays. See this week's menu online at www.sobrogrill.com or call 615-254-9060.

Tom Morales is called the "caterer to the stars," having provided meals for more than 400 movie sets, and garnering the praise of Meg Ryan, Gwyneth Paltrow, Bill Murray, and Jodie Foster, to name a few. Tom's Nashville location at 408 Broadway can provide catering for private or corporate events in the area. Visit TomKats Incorporated at www.tomkats.com online for more details. For more information, call 615-256-9596 or 800-322-9591.

LILLIE BELLE'S OF FRANKLIN

Be sure and check out Lillie Belle's of Franklin at 132 Third Ave. S. See page 204 for full details.

TRUMPS

Trumps is a full-service hair salon and day spa that is known for pampering. In addition to hair coloring, hair styling, massage, microdermabrasion and airbrush tanning, owner Earl Cox offers a variety of quality skin and hair care products like N.V. Perricone, Barex, Aeto and Phytologie. Trumps, 4010 Hillsboro Cir. in Nashville, is open 8 am-6 pm Tuesday and Thursday, 8 am-4 pm Wednesday and Friday and Saturday from 8 am-2 pm. Call 615-385-9898.

TIBA
DE NUHAD KHOURY
Spa • Parfumerie • Accessories • Gifts

Tiba is a glorious, sensuously textured oasis in the midst of a hectic stress-filled world. Escape to Tiba, where the great health and beauty regimens of Europe, America, and Asia await you. Explore Tiba's Institute of Traditional Oriental Medicine, and meet some of the finest international health experts in a warm, friendly atmosphere. Tiba offers a brilliantly chosen array of services, including: massage, mineral baths, mud wraps, hydrotherapy, microdermabrasion, acupuncture, hair design, laser hair removal, photorejuvenation and more. It's no wonder Tiba has garnered rave reviews in *Vogue*, *Elle*, *Harper's Bazaar*, *Glamour* and *Southern Living*. Discover what Tiba already knows—you deserve the best. Tiba, located at 2126 Abbott Martin Rd., #132 in The Mall at Green Hills, is open Monday-Friday 10 am-9 pm, Saturday until 8 pm and Sunday 1-6 pm. Call 615-269-5121, 800-964-6868, or visit www.tibaspa.com. *(Color photo featured in front section of book.)*

Private Edition

Private Edition has grown from 888 square feet to 6,000 square feet since 1981 and the name Private Edition has become known worldwide. Linda Roberts, the "cosmetic guru of Nashville," has taken the make-up and skin-care world by storm with her very successful "Therapy Systems" line. You will find these products, as well as coveted name brands such as Trish McEvoy, Kiehls, and Laura Mercier, at Private Edition, 4009 Hillsboro Rd. in Nashville. (Don't be surprised if you see a few of Nashville's rich and famous like Reese Witherspoon, Ashley Judd and Faith Hill who frequent the store!) While in Nashville, don't miss Linda's newest creation, The Cosmetic Market and Take Out Café. Call 615-292-8606 or visit www.privateeditioninc.com online. Open Monday through Saturday 9:30 am-5:30 pm.

Jubilee Singers of Fisk University in Nashville introduced to the world the plaintive beauty and tradition of the Negro spiritual, which became the basis for other genres of African–American music. It was because of their successful tours throughout America and Europe to raise funds for the university during the 1870s that Nashville first became known for its music.

DISCOVER CHATTANOOGA/ SIGNAL MOUNTAIN

CHATTANOOGA

"*All Aboard*!" It has been called "the scenic city," "a Top-10 Dream Town," "Top Family Vacation Spot," and "one cool city!" Chattanooga, Tennessee, is an incredible combination of family fun, history, outdoor adventure, and romantic escapes—a perfect vacation destination.

It is called "scenic" because the beauty of the area will literally take your breath away. Thick forests and limestone caverns, underground waterfalls and beautiful mountains provide a timeless splendor to this vibrant city. You'll find hiking trails, fishing piers, parks, rivers, byways, and skyways for every kind of outdoor entertainment you can imagine.

For Namesake

The name Chattanooga is a Creek Indian word for "rock coming to a point." This refers to Lookout Mountain, which begins in Chattanooga and stretches 88 miles through Georgia and Alabama. The city was once called Lookout Point, and before that, Ross's Landing. Established by John Ross, Chief of the Cherokee Indians in 1816, Ross's Landing served as the center for the Cherokee trade business. When the Cherokee parties left Ross's Landing for the West on the "Trail of Tears," the city officially took the name Chattanooga.

Outdoor Beauty

The mountains and valleys of Chattanooga come alive for visitors who take the Lookout Mountain Incline Railway ride through "America's Most Amazing Mile." The breathtaking 72.7 percent grade of the track near the top makes the Incline the steepest passenger railway in the world! As you climb historic Lookout Mountain, you can see the Great Smoky Mountains, which are actually more than 100 miles away.

Because of Chattanooga's beautiful mountains and the moderate climate, this area has become the hang gliding capital of the East and home to America's largest hang gliding mountain school. The area is also famous for its wonderful caverns and caves, which are awesome to explore. Raccoon Mountain Caverns were carved from pure limestone, formed on the bottom of an ancient sea. The tours are exciting and educational, and the kiddos will love being able to pan for gemstones!

All Aboard!

The City of Chattanooga has so many wonderful things to see and experience, but the first thing most people want to do when they arrive is to—you guessed it—see the "Chattanooga Choo Choo!" (You're singing the song right now, aren't you?) It is, after all, what made this Tennessee city famous. You'll feel as though you've stepped back in time when you board the Chattanooga Choo Choo and have dinner in a Victorian railcar, or you can ride through a pre-Civil War tunnel pulled by a steam locomotive. Chattanooga became part of the golden age of railroads during the early 1900s, and Woodrow Wilson, Teddy Roosevelt, William Jennings Bryant, and Franklin D. Roosevelt were just a few of the millions of travelers who passed through the city during the 61 years the depot was operative. The last train left Chattanooga in 1970, and the depot was boarded up and left to ruin. Happily, a group of investors restored and renovated the depot, and the Chattanooga Choo Choo opened as a historic hotel. Remember the 1941 #1 hit song made famous by the King of Swing, Glenn Miller? (The one you were just humming…) Well, you'll hear the "Chattanooga Choo Choo" song quite often during your stay here.

Then and Now

Chattanooga has grown and changed dramatically through the years. Over a century ago, it was a strategic location during the Civil War, as well as a major rail center. During World War II, the famous Choo Choo brought fame to the city. Forty years later the community held visioning sessions and developed programs that brought revitalization to the riverfront and downtown area. Public and private partnerships built on Chattanooga's assets—her natural beauty and fascinating history—creating parks, trails, and world-class attractions. Before long, more than 28,000 readers of *Southern Living Magazine* had voted Chattanooga a top choice as a favorite place to dine, play, visit and stay. In fact, the *Washington Post* says that the city is "on its way to becoming the prettiest city for its size in America!"

One of the top attractions in the city is the world's largest fresh-water aquarium, The Tennessee Aquarium, which is home to 9,000 animals. With 60-foot canyons, living forests, and beautiful water-falls, the Aquarium takes you on a trip from a mountain forest to the Gulf of Mexico. You'll see sharks, stingrays, and schools of colorful fish, tiny seahorses, and whimsical sea dragons. Experience the forest and feel the spray of a cascading waterfall, and visit the Amazon exhibit where piranhas swim with anacondas.

Plan to spend time in Chattanooga's beautiful Coolidge Park, named for World War II Medal of Honor recipient, Charles B. Coolidge. The six-acre park features antique carousel horses, an interactive fountain, the world's longest pedestrian bridge, a rock climbing wall, unique shops, delightful restaurants, and riverboat rides.

Along with all of the adventure, history, and exciting attractions in Chattanooga, you'll find an array of cultural and artistic diversions. Museums, theaters, art galleries, and musical productions bring the music and personality of the city to life. Downtown Chattanooga is filled with unique shops and restaurants that attract visitors from across the state, and the city's annual festivals and celebrations are legendary.

In the spring of 2005, the city completes its 21st Century Waterfront Development Plan. This ambitious and transformative project brings expansions to the Tennessee Aquarium, Hunter Museum of American Art and Riverfront Parkway. The $120 million project also results in a renovation of the Children's Discovery Museum and creates a passageway from the Tennessee Aquarium to the Tennessee River. Construction of a pedestrian bridge, walkways and access roads makes it easier for ladies on their day out to make their way to the city's downtown attractions.

We hope you have lots of time to spend in this remarkable city; to enjoy her beauty and charm, to learn her history, to explore the shops and to meet the wonderful people who own them. You're going to fall in love with Chattanooga, and agree with the locals who say, "The Attraction's Only Natural!" (Don't be surprised if you find yourself singing "that Choo Choo song" all day!)

SIGNAL MOUNTAIN

Just a few very beautiful miles from the "big city" of Chattanooga lies this sweet little town called Signal Mountain. It is located on what is known as Walden's Ridge (or in the earliest days, Walling Settlement). Prior to this settlement, there were only a few Indians living in the valley below the mountain. Before the Civil War, it is believed that the Creek and Cherokee Indians used to send fire and smoke signals from what came to be called "Signal Point." Then, during the Civil War, the Union Army used Signal Point as a communication station to contact Union locations in the Chattanooga area. During this time, there were only a few families living in Walden's Ridge, but when cholera struck Chattanooga in 1873, many families headed for the open spaces of the mountain. The town of Signal Mountain actually began when visionary Charles E. James purchased 4,400 acres in the area so that he and his family could escape the 1878 yellow fever epidemic. History books tell us that he had huge plans for the mountain area: for railroads, dams, towns, and a fine hotel on the top of the mountain. By 1913, 12 miles of streetcar track had been completed, connecting Signal Mountain to Chattanooga. The Signal Mountain Hotel opened in 1913—complete with casino and dance floors!

Although the town has grown and changed over the years, it was not to become the grand metropolis that Mr. James had envisioned. Today, Signal Mountain is still a small, quaint, and charming town that has retained the serenity and peacefulness that attracted the earliest settlers—a beautiful and special place to visit. The townspeople are extremely friendly and welcoming, and the shopping opportunities are wonderful. You'll find great antique stores and restaurants, recreational activities, and family fun entertainment.

For more information about Chattanooga, contact the Chattanooga Convention and Visitors Bureau at 800-332-3344, 423-424-4430 or visit www.chattanoogafun.com online. Or, contact the Chattanooga Area Chamber of Commerce at www.chattanoogachamber.com online or call 423-756-2121.

For more information about Signal Mountain, contact the Town of Signal Mountain at 423-886-2177.

Chattanooga
Fairs Festivals & Fun

January
    Rock City's Enchanted Garden of Lights
    Deck the Falls
    Dive into Winter

February
    Taste of Chattanooga
    Valentine Dinner Cruise
    Valentine Special Rail Excursion to Chickamauga
    Dive intoWinter

April
    Spring Wildflower Festival & Native Plant Sale
    Tour of Downtown Living
    Chattanooga Market (April-December)
    Traditional Jazz Festival

May
    Traditional Jazz Festival
    Bessie Smith Traditional Jazz Festival
    Southside Block Party
    Nightfall Concert Series (May-September)
    Rhythm & Noon Concert Series (May-August)
    Four Bridges Arts Festival
    River Roast

June
    Riverbend Festival

July
    Pops on the River

August
    Southern Brewers Festival

September
Swingfest
CultureFest
Alabama Tennessee Trail of Tears Ride
Wine Over Water
Rock City's Enchanted Maize Maze (September-November)
Hamilton County Fair
Bluegrass Experience

October
Bluegrass Experience
Boo at the Zoo
Prater's Mill County Fair
Ketner's Mill Country Fair
Fall Leaf Cruises
Fall Color Cruise and Folk Festival
Autumn Steam Excursions
Wine Over Water

November
Rock City's Enchanted Garden of Lights
Ruby Falls' Deck the Falls
Dive into Winter
Christmas Carol Dinner Cruises
Christmas on the River and Grande Illumination
Breakfast with Santa

December
Holiday Starlight Parade
Appalachian Christmas Concert
Rock City's Enchanted Garden of Lights
Ruby Falls' Deck the Falls
Dive into Winter
Christmas Carol Dinner Cruises
Christmas Candelight Tours
Holiday Lights
Chattanooga Choo Choo's Victorian Nights
Christmas on the River
New Year's Eve Dinner Cruise
 New Year at Noon

Signal Mountain Fairs Festivals & Fun

January
> Red Hat Appreciation Month
> The Mountain Opry (monthly)

February
> Signal Mountain Play House Winter Production
> "Mugs for the Heart" at Mole Hill Pottery

March
> Saint Patrick's Day "Lucky Draw"

April
> Alexian Village Egg Hunt
> Dogwood Celebration

May
> Plant Swap
> Shackleford Ridge Wildflower Trail Tours
> Mountain Arts Community Center Shrimp Boil

June
> The Garden Tour

July
> The 4th All Day Family Fun & Fireworks
> Signal Mountain Play House Summer Production
> The Brow Gallery Christmas in July Sale

August
> The World's Longest Yard Sale

September

Labor Day Lion's Club BBQ & All Day Family Fun
Mole Hill Pottery "2nds Show & Sale"
Halkwatch at Signal Point Park
"Hike Against Hunger"

October

Holiday Hodge Podge
"Haunted Fire Hall"
Stump, Jump, Run 5K
Mountain Arts Community Center Murder Mystery
Alexian Halloween Party

November

Best Christmas Pageant Ever
"Sunday on Signal"

December

"A Lady's Day Out" Holiday Recognition
Signal Crest Church Live Nativity
Signal Mountain Christmas Train

Antiques, Artists & Art Galleries

NORTHGATE GALLERY, INC.

Opened in 1968 by David and the late Brenda Patterson, Northgate Gallery, 5520 Hwy. 153 in Hixson, continues to be one of the largest antiques and furnishings showrooms in the area. As a direct importer for English and French antiques and custom-made reproductions, the gallery includes a complete source of fine European antiques for the collector, dealer, or interior designer. The inventory changes monthly as new shipments arrive from England, Scotland, and France. Northgate Gallery is also a leading auction gallery in the South, specializing in liquidating estates and collections of antiques and fine furnishings. Monthly auctions are conducted at the showroom, but on-site estate auctions can also be scheduled. The gallery is open Monday-Friday 8 am-5 pm, or you may visit the second location in the Nashville/Brentwood area. Visit www.northgateantiques.com online or call 423-877-6114.

Whether you are looking for a wonderful antique, a fountain for your patio, an unusual lamp, an original oil painting, or a great hand-painted chest, you are sure to find it here! The Galleries at Southside, 1404 Cowart St., is located downtown, just blocks from the Chattanooga Choo-Choo and the Tennessee Aquarium. You'll find more than 50 dealers, offering decorative accessories, gifts, collectibles, rugs, garden statuary, jewelry and more. Their Christopher Radko store has recently been designated one of the 100 Premiere Dealers and given special "Rising Star" status. While you are here, take time to enjoy lunch or an afternoon dessert in the European café. Hours are Monday-Saturday 10 am to 6 pm. Call 423-267-8101 or visit www.thegalleries-southside.com online.

Partners Connie Knox and Jim Althaus represent many combined years of experience in the antique business and have had a major impact on the development of Chattanooga's up and coming "Southside." Southside Antiques, located at 1401-C Williams St., has been an anchor store in the area for more than eight years. The gallery offers an extensive inventory of personally selected 18th and 19th century American, English, and French antiques. You'll find furniture, lamps, silver, oriental rugs, art, and decorative accessories. In addition to the owners' antiques, there are nine prominent antique dealers represented in the 3,000-square-foot historic building. The store is open Tuesday-Saturday 10 am-5 pm and Sunday and Monday by appointment. Call 423-265-3004.

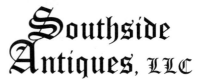

Churches Antiques & Estate Pieces

Don't leave Signal Mountain without a visit to Churches Antiques and Estate Pieces at 1819 Taft Hwy. The experience will be "heavenly." The antique store is located within an old church at the top of the mountain. The historic church is now filled with beautiful and unique antique pieces including furniture, estate jewelry, silver, china and vintage linens. The atmosphere is wonderful—a quiet, peaceful place that is the perfect setting for beautiful pieces

from the past. Owner Lois Killebrew is a charming and vivacious woman who is passionate about Signal Mountain and the people who call it home. She always has something exciting planned to bring the community together, like antique roadshows, where experts in many fields identify and evaluate unknown treasures for customers. You will love meeting Lois and her friendly staff and appreciate their knowledge of antiques. The entire place is so charming and such a fun place to shop. In the lower level of Churches Antiques, you'll find a quaint little coffee shop called "Heavenly Grounds." Enjoy a cup of gourmet coffee, a cappuccino, latte or mocha and then browse the antiques to your heart's content. For information, call 423-886-9636.

If you fall in love with Churches Antiques (and you will) Lois can also help you find the perfect property to call your own. She's the owner of Mountain City Realtors, and has been serving the people of Signal Mountain and the greater Chattanooga area for more than 30 years. A licensed Realtor since 1971 she has been very active in the community. "My love is matching people with that perfect home," she confides. As a Multi-Million Dollar Producer, Lois offers experience and knowledge of the area to provide the best service available to her clients. Call 423-886-1300 x202 or visit www.mountaincityrealtors.com online.

Lambs & Ivy

Antiques • Accessories • Gifts

"Mairzy doats and dozy doats, and liddle lamzy divey. A kiddlely divey too, wouldn't you?" Remember this funny song of the 40s? It was the inspiration for the name of Barbie Bynum's wonderful antique and collectible shop at 1306 Hanover St. in Chattanooga's Riverview area. If you played with Patsy, Shirley Temple, Toni, Dimples, Ginny dolls, Madame Alexander's little women, Wendy, Cissy and Cissette, or 1960s Barbie and Midge; if you love old quilts, needlepoint, and antique furniture; if "Gone With The Wind" is your all-time favorite movie; Lambs & Ivy is an absolute must! From its cozy front porch filled with decorative accessories, to the rooms filled with antique furniture, jewelry, and vintage collectibles, you are certain to "buy back" a memory. The shop is open Monday-Saturday 10 am-5:30 pm. For more information, contact Barbie at 423-756-7200, (and make her sing the song for you!)

MOLE HILL POTTERY

When Kathy Owens began making her pottery more than 25 years ago, she saw little molehills popping up all over the backyard through the window of her studio. Since moles are very "earthy," like her clay, Mole Hill Pottery seemed the perfect name! Today you'll find a wide collection of folk, traditional, contemporary, and raku pottery in an array of glaze colors. There are more than 1,000 national artists represented at this beautiful gallery. Mole Hill features everything from garden art, blown glass, and jewelry to baskets and wooden art. Works displayed in the gallery are all hand-crafted in the USA—truly a treat for the senses! Mole Hill Pottery, 1210 Taft Hwy. in Signal Mountain, is open Monday-Saturday 9:30 am-8 pm and Sunday 1-6 pm. Call 423-886-5636.

VINTAGE WARES
FOR THE
HOME & GARDEN

Antique lovers take note! Chattanooga is the destination for antique and collectible treasure hunting at Knitting Mill Antiques, 205 Manufacturers Rd. With over 100 dealers occupying 20,000 square feet, this beautifully refurbished old building has taken on a new life with the finest selection of vintage wares in southeastern Tennessee. Don't expect the rows of clutter you find at many antique malls; owners Lynn and Scott Short have kept the mall open, accessible and interesting. Says Lynn, "We have been dedicated to offering true antiques to our customers. We also have a wide date-range of items, from period pieces to mid-century modern. There is something here for everyone." The mall has its own parking and is wonderfully climate controlled. Don't miss this one! It's worth the trip. And while there, be sure to check out the photograph of the Finishing Department employees of 1927! Open 10 am-6 pm Monday-Saturday and noon-5 pm Sunday. Call 423-267-1922.

**Finishing Department
1927**

Anna Ball White

When Anna Ball White opened her store in 1956, she was indeed a pioneer in the world of "women in business." She began sewing at age 6, was an accomplished seamstress by her teen years, and turned a home-based industry into a very successful ladies' clothing store. Anna Ball White, though in her 90s, is still an integral part of the wonderful boutique that bears her name. When her daughter Trish Foy joined her during the 80s, they relocated to 2021 Hamilton Place Blvd., and continue to be one of Chattanooga's most loved places to shop.

They carry wonderful, up-scale lines of designer casual wear and sports wear, as well as unique accessories and jewelry. Anna Ball White is open Monday-Saturday 10 am-5 pm. For more information, call 423-499-4940.

It's the best "shopping for two!" Located in Chattanooga's trendy Southside, Bellies & Babies, 1428 Williams St., Ste. A, offers a fresh new approach to maternity fashion and unique items for children and infants. Creative and energetic owners April Watson and Caroline Williams want expectant mothers to feel as beautiful on the outside as they do on the inside, which is why they offer items from the hottest designers from around the world. Today's mothers-to-be can now choose from exciting and fashionable separates, jackets, work out clothes, sleepwear, and accessories—even strapless dresses and lace pants for special dressy events. For the beautiful "new addition," you'll find unique clothing, furniture, bedding and gifts. Open Monday-Friday 10 am-5 pm and Saturday until 3 pm. Call 423-267-7888.

Shopping Susanna*s at 921 Barton Ave. is a special treat. This wonderful ladies boutique is located in a 1920s bungalow in the heart of Riverview, one of Chattanooga's most prestigious neighborhoods. Owners, Charlotte White, and sisters Katherine Roberts and Janet Hartman, are friends who just happen to make great business partners. They carry exclusive lines by Marc Jacobs, LaFayette 148, Womyn, Juicy Couture, Seven for all Mankind, Pink Tartan, and many more wonderful names. Their clientele ranges from teen to "queen," and the clothes and accessories make every customer feel confident and beautiful. Customer service is a first priority at Susanna*s—they want your experience to be warm and inviting, like visiting with a friend! This store will beckon to you again and again. Stop by Tuesday-Friday 10 am-6 pm and Saturday 11 am-4 pm. For more information, call 423-265-4777.

FLOWERS BY GIL & CURT

Walk into the showroom of Flowers by Gil & Curt at 206 Tremont St. in Chattanooga, and find yourself surrounded by an eclectic array of designer accessories, antiques, floral designs, and gift ideas. Order invitations, browse through the upscale linen selections, or spend time selecting just the right item for your home. Whether planning an elaborate wedding or celebrating the mundane, the earthy style of Flowers by Gil & Curt will help you create the perfect backdrop.

Dedicated to making your experience a pleasant one, Flowers by Gil & Curt always goes the extra mile to make your floral gift perfect. Stop by Monday-Friday 8:30 am-5 pm and Saturday until noon. Call 800-336-0218, 423-756-8603 or shop seven days a week by visiting www.gilandcurt.com online.

THE CLAY POT

This beautiful floral and gift boutique will be one of your very favorite Chattanooga "discoveries." The Clay Pot, 1311 Hanover St., is located in a charming 1930s bungalow, and is known for its creative displays, with unique colors and products. Owner Joe Jumper specializes in exquisite, very natural creations using beautiful blooms mixed with colorful fruit, berries, and greenery. You'll find fresh flowers, garden baskets, orchid plants, custom silk arrangements, unique gifts, and home accessories. Some of the "Clay Pot" favorites are the Rose Mounds—beautiful roses mounded in terra cotta pots; Cube Vases—filled tightly with an assortment of short, compact flowers; Phalaenopsis Orchids; Votivo Red Currant Candles; and of course, the adorable white mixed breed mutt "Littlebit," who loves belly rubs! The shop is open Monday-Friday 10 am-5 pm and Saturday until 2 pm. Call 423-265-2007.

The Brow Gallery

After living in Europe during the 1960s and shopping everywhere, Connie Blunt knew exactly the type of shop she wanted to open "back home" in Signal Mountain. The Brow Gallery, 1221 Taft Hwy., is a full-service gift and accessories shop. It is honored to be an official Colonial Williamsburg Gift Shop, a Virginia Metalcrafters Gift Gallery, and a designated Arthur Court Gallery. Her bridal registry lines include Wedgwood, Mottahedah, Royal Worchester, Present Tense, Spode, Vietri, Portmeirion, and more. You'll also find wonderful collectibles such as Dept. 56 and Byers Choice Carolers, as well as bath and body products by Aromatique, Lady Primrose, Thymes, and Crabtree and Evelyn. Stop by Monday-Saturday 9:30 am-5:30 pm. For information, call 423-886-5973.

signal mtn.
nursery
AND LANDSCAPING

The scenic drive to the top of Signal Mountain yields one of the most marvelous treats that the gardener or artistic soul could ever desire. At the end of a wooded road is an incredible nursery that is reminiscent of one of the South's finest botanical gardens.

Visitors to the 10-acre nursery tell owners Laurel and David Steele that they are surprised they are not charged admission to view the grounds. Upon entering the greenhouse, you are overwhelmed by the magnitude and opulence of all the flowers and plants. The intense colors, along with the soothing sounds of the many fountains throughout the nursery, surprise and delight the senses.

Laurel and David grow at least 90 percent of their inventory in their 46 greenhouses, so they are able to maintain the exceptional high quality in their plants, which has drawn gardeners from as far away as Birmingham and Atlanta for more than 27 years. They offer a wide variety of ornamental shrubs and trees, over 25,000 perennials, unique groundcovers, spectacular annuals, and a huge array of seasonal plants such as pansies, mums and poinsettias. The staff members are knowledgeable with growth habits, season of bloom, soil treatment, etc., and they are always eager to assist with plant selection and landscape design.

Before you leave the nursery, be sure to spend some time in the gift shop where you'll find all the gardening essentials, as well as a large variety of decorative items to give your home and garden a personal flair.

Whether you are a "weekend gardener" or a "professional," a visit to Signal Mtn. Nursery, located at 1100 Hubbard Rd., will be a wonderful experience. The nursery is open Monday-Friday, 8 am-5 pm and Saturday 9 am-5 pm with extended seasonal hours. For more information, call 423-886-3174.

The Flowering Pot

Judy Kazemersky's love of nature, gardening, and all things green led her to open this amazing garden and gift shop at 1904 Taft Hwy. One of the most special places in Signal Mountain, The Flowering Pot is located in a charming green and white 1915 cottage, which still has the original stone fireplace and stone walkway. Four cozy rooms are filled with fine tools, garden art, architectural elements, birdhouses and feeders, bat and butterfly houses, and

even fiber nesting pouches for wrens and chickadees. There is an abundance of wonderful gift items, such as copper-wrapped glass gazing balls, wind chimes, outside clocks, as well as yummy candles. The Flowering Pot is a gardener's dream! It is open Tuesday-Saturday 10 am-5 pm. Call 423-886-9246.

Coca-Cola was first bottled in 1899 at a plant on Patten Pkwy. downtown Chattanooga after two local attorneys purchased the bottling rights to the drink for $1.

Gourmet, Specialty Foods, Ice Cream Parlors & Tearooms

If you have never had the pleasure of taking a true "British Tea," you have missed one of life's most elegant pleasures. Chattanoogans are extremely happy that Angela Becksvoort found her way from a British colony in Africa to their Southern town, and especially glad that she has brought them the pleasure of The English Rose. She established this authentic British tearoom in 1997 in the foyer of the original Grand Hotel at 1401 Market St. It's no wonder this exquisite tearoom has been featured in several publications such as *Southern Living Mag-*

azine. Angela says, "We strive to graciously bring the timeless traditions of England to the South in an elegant but relaxed setting." Lunch is served from 11 am -3 pm, and tea is served all day from 10 am-5:30 pm. Call 423-265-5900.

Opened in 1999 by the son of a third-generation candy maker, Clumpies Ice Cream Co. makes every flavor in-house. *Southern Living*, *Atlanta Journal Constitution*, and the people of Chattanooga agree that you cannot fully experience the unique flavor of Chattanooga without sampling this local treat. Located at 26B Frazier Ave. downtown next to Coolidge Park Carousel. For more information, call 423-267-5425 (LICK) or visit www.clumpies.com online.

SOMETHING SWEET

If you have a sweet tooth, Something Sweet, 1210 Taft Hwy., will be your favorite place on Signal Mountain. Kari McCleery offers 20 varieties of fudge, specialty children's candy, fudge-dipped strawberries, and her award-winning Pecan Turtles—voted best in Taste of Chattanooga. She even ships throughout the United States and abroad! Hours are Wednesday-Friday noon-5:30 pm. Visit www.somethingsweet.us online or call 423-886-1896.

Hotels

CHATTANOOGA I-75

Whether you are traveling with a group of ladies on a fun day out, the entire family, or on a corporate business trip, you'll find everything you could possibly need here—the Courtyard by Marriott in Chattanooga, 2210 Bams Dr. This is a beautiful hotel with a bright lobby and an extremely friendly staff. The hotel is within walking distance of Tennessee's largest indoor mall, The Hamilton Place Mall, and several superb restaurants. In fact, more than 30 restaurants can be found within a quarter of a mile of the hotel. You can also take in a movie at one of the nearby 17 movie theaters or drive only 15 minutes to Chattanooga's exciting downtown area.

Guests may choose from King or Queen rooms or suites. All of the suites feature a separate living area with a mini-fridge, and some with Jacuzzis. All rooms are equipped with cable, HBO, and Direct Video service. You will appreciate in-room coffee service for that very important "first cup of the morning." The rooms come equipped with hair dryers, irons and ironing boards, and there are two telephones with modems and a work desk in each room—perfect for business travelers. If you are a frequent corporate traveler, be sure to ask about their special corporate rates. If you need to schedule a conference or business seminar, you can take advantage of the meeting room, which can accommodate as many as 40 people.

One of the best features the Courtyard by Marriott offers is the complete Southern breakfast served each morning. It's not the typical complimentary continental; it is a full hot breakfast. After a long day of shopping or enjoying the fascinating sights and adventures of Chattanooga, you will love the special way you are treated here at the Courtyard. The staff takes great pride in its customer service. Visit www.marriott.com/CHACH online or call 423-499-4400 or 800-228-9290. *(Color photo featured in front section of book.)*

Jewelry

 The wonderful display of fine jewelry in the 11 windows includes exclusive lines from David Yurman and John Hardy, but these exquisite treasures are just the frosting on the cake! Fischer Evans, 801 Market St., is one of Chattanooga's most remarkable stores, and has been a part of the city's history since 1869! In addition to jewelry, you'll find china, crystal and silver. It is the exclusive dealer for many fine lines such as Baccarat, Lynn Chase, Herend, and Christofle. And, if you're looking for beautiful antique and estate pieces of jewelry, silver, porcelains and fine paper and stationery by Crane and William Arthur, you're in luck! Fischer Evans promises and delivers unparalleled customer service, so stop by Monday-Friday 10 am-5:30 pm. Call 423-267-0901 or 800-288-4807.

Pampered Pets

THE BONE APPETIT BAKERY
GOURMET TREATS AND BOUTIQUE FOR PETS

Even the most pampered pet will find something to bow/meow about when they visit The Bone Appetit Bakery, 103 Frazier Ave. The bakery opened in 1999—the first of its kind in Chattanooga—and has been a delightful success. With treats like Scooby Scoops, Russell Rover Bon Bons, and Betty Cocker Brownies, it's no surprise this place is such a "doggoned" hit. Teddy, the resident Yorkie supervises, but all canine (and feline) visitors are invited to "taste test" the new treats. You'll also find whimsical jewelry and accessories, bejeweled collars and leashes, and high-flying Frisbees. There is even a pet spa facility on the premises called "Groomingdales," where Fifi can get her hair done, her nails trimmed, and even a massage! Visit Monday-Saturday 10 am-6 pm and Sunday 1-5 pm. Call 423-756-2663

Just across the river from the Tennessee Aquarium in the North Shore, you'll find Chattanooga's own little bit of Ireland, at Durty Nelly's, A Grand Irish Pub and Restaurant. Chattanooga's only Irish pub was opened in 1992 by noted Washington, D.C. publican and restauranteur, Denis Brady and his wife Wynne. Now living in Chattanooga, the Bradys can be found most any day greeting guests and overseeing operations at 109 N. Market St. Durty Nelly's has built a reputation for unsurpassed food quality and customer service specializing in Irish-American fare such as Shepherd's Pie, Fish and Chips, and Scottish Bangers and Mash, as well as American favorites like Murphy's Pot Roast and great hamburgers. For a complete menu and photos of the pub, visit www.durtypub.com online or call 423-265-9970 for more information. Open Monday-Friday 11 am and Saturday noon until everyone goes home!

WAYCRAZY'S
Bar-B-Que

First Lady Laura Bush feasted on Waycrazy's Bar-B-Que aboard Airforce One. You will have to visit this Signal Mountain restaurant at 3720 Taft Hwy. to sample the unforgettable hand-pulled, hickory-smoked specialties. The unique name was a college nickname for the original owner, the late Michael Waycaster, who started barbecuing here in 1988. Waycrazy's Bar-B-Que is a delightful find. Open Monday-Saturday 11 am-8 pm. Call 423-886-3283. Eat in, carryout, and catering available.

Cibo!

It is both sleekly modern and contemporary, yet warm and inviting, and it is one of Chattanooga's most respected eateries. Cibo! could just as easily be at home in the heart of Manhattan, yet the personal attention and friendliness of the staff is "truly Tennessee!" Cibo! is located within walking distance of the downtown hotels at 850 Market Street, on Miller Plaza, home of Nightfall—a free summer concert series that takes place each Friday 6 pm-dark, June through September.

The interior is very unique and sophisticated, featuring one-of-a-kind charcoal-on-canvas drawings of old Mediterranean buildings and walkways, a concrete bar, and blonde wood floors. Cibo! offers Chattanooga's best Mediterranean and Italian cuisine, as well as delicious  Spanish, Greek, French and Middle Eastern entrees. Each season the menu is revitalized with new dishes and entrees. Cibo! always uses fresh ingredients and even has fresh fish delivered daily! There is always something to satisfy everyone, including fish, veal, shrimp, chicken, chops and steaks. Cibo! has a full bar with imported beers and over 100 wines from California, Portugal, Chile, Italy, Spain, Australia, France, New Zealand, and Germany with Happy Hour Monday-Friday 4:30-7 pm, featuring discounted well drinks and domestic beers, and nightly wine specials. A semi-private dining room is available for special occasions and can accommodate up to 35.

Hours are Monday-Thursday 5-10 pm. and Friday-Saturday until 11 pm. Call 423-267-7141 for Cibo!

Sharon

Catering to everyone from office workers to celebrities, brother and sister team Sharon McMurry and Shawn Smith have carved quite a niche for themselves in Chattanooga. They are the owner and manager of Sharon, 415 N. Market St. Sharon is a master colorist who looks at hair the way a painter sees a blank canvas, and the entire staff is very friendly and knowledgeable. The salon is open Tuesday-Saturday 10 am-6 pm. Call 423-634-1920 for an appointment.

DISCOVER
BELL BUCKLE

What a delightful name for such a charming town! Historic Bell Buckle, Tennessee, embodies all of the slow-moving, sweetness of the South and has been able to retain the innocence and beauty of its early history. Visitors use adjectives such as "charming," "unique," and "quaint," to describe Bell Buckle. This turn-of-the-century railroad town has a definite Victorian flavor.

History at a Glance

There are several legends as to how this town got its unusual name. One legend tells of a wandering cow that wandered a bit too close to an Indian, who killed it, and then took the cow's bell and tied it with a buckle around a tree as a warning to the settlers to keep their cows home. Other stories say that Indians carved a bell and a buckle on a tree as a warning to settlers about their wandering cows. A third legend says that early surveyors used markings to indicate uses for the land. A bell and a buckle meant "good pastureland for cows." No one knows for sure how this wonderful town got its name…besides, the various legends just add to the mysterious charm of Bell Buckle.

The town of Bell Buckle grew up around its first railroad depot, which was built in 1853 near the "beech tree" that displayed the first bell and buckle, according to legend. The town prospered, and the railroad enabled Bell Buckle to serve as a major stockyard between Nashville and Chattanooga. The town was the scene of many troop movements during the Civil War and fared well until the Great Depression. Throughout the hard years, however, the town drew upon the strength of her most precious asset—the townspeople. The *Bell Buckle Echo*, a local newspaper said, "The farm ladies who knitted, quilted, and made flour sack dresses saw the kinship of creativity in those who painted, made stained glass and pottery." During the early 1970s, a rebirth began which revitalized the historic downtown area, turning Bell Buckle, Tennessee, into a shopper's dream. If you're in the market for unusual antiques, hand-made crafts, country cooking, and fun festivals, then Bell Buckle is for you.

Something for Everyone

One of the town's most famous citizens, Anne White-Scruggs, has laughingly said that Bell Buckle is "progressively backwards." The trains still whistle through town, and visitors come from near and far to sample true Tennessee hospitality in this picture postcard town. With events like Daffodil Day in March; the RC & Moon Pie Festival in June; the Quilt Tour in September; and the not-to-be-missed Webb School Art and Craft Festival in October; there is always something wonderful planned for your visit. RC Colas and Moon Pies? Doesn't that bring back good memories?

For more than 20 years, the Bell Buckle Chamber of Commerce events are always the third Saturday of the month. For additional information about Bell Buckle, contact the Chamber of Commerce at 931-389-9663 or visit www.bellbucklechamber.com online. Or, contact the Bell Buckle Association of Merchants by visiting www.bellbuckletn.org online or calling 931-389-BELL. *(Color photo featured in front section of book.)*

Bell Buckle Fairs Festivals & Fun

March
Daffodil Day

May
Mayfest

June
RC & Moon Pie Festival
1st Community Bank's RC/Moon Pie 10 Miler

September
Walking Quilt Tour

October
Webb School Art & Craft Festival
An Old Fashioned Haunted Evening

December
Christmas In Bell Buckle

Step into this charming ice cream parlor and antique store at 15 E. Webb Rd. in Bell Buckle, and you'll step back in time 100 years! The store features "tone-on-tone" vignettes of timeless antique treasures, primitives, architectural fragments, garden elements, and of course, delicious, hand-dipped ice cream with all the toppings! Hours are Monday-Saturday 9 am-5 pm and Sunday noon-5 pm. For more information, call 931-389-6549 or visit online www.bellbucklechamber.com.

Bell Buckle Antique & Craft Mall

Linda Key was the county's first female mayor, and has been in office for three terms, but she has been in the antique business for more than 30 years! She owns the Bell Buckle Antique and Craft Mall at 112 Main St. Browse to your heart's content through 40 booths of antiques, collectibles, quilts, linens, and antique glassware. Hours are Monday-Saturday 10 am-5 pm and Sunday 1-5 pm. For more information, visit www.bellbuckleantiques.com online or call 931-389-6174.

BELL BUCKLE BED & BREAKFAST

AND

POTTERY STUDIO

This 19th century Victorian B&B offers lovely rooms with private baths and cable, as well as Anne White-Scruggs' pottery at 17 Webb Rd. in Bell Buckle. The front porch wicker swing begs for company and decorative art is everywhere. For more information, about Bell Buckle Bed and Breakfast and Pottery, call 931-389-9371. *(Color photo featured in front section of book.)*

and Music Parlour

You'll get more than a great meal at the family-owned-and-operated Bell Buckle Café. Located in a 125-year-old former post office at 16 Railroad Sq., you might just be the first to hear the next country music superstar! Enjoy the most delicious hickory smoked BBQ and hamburgers, and hear musicians perform country, jazz, and bluegrass during the weekends. (Be sure to try the Homemade Oatmeal Cake with Hot Caramel Topping!) Visit www.bellbucklecafe.com online, or call 931-389-9693. Hours are Monday 8 am-2 pm, Tuesday-Thursday until 8 pm, Friday-Saturday until 9 pm, and Sunday 11 am-5 pm.

BRIDLEWOOD FARM

Bridlewood Farm, Hwy. 82 E. in Bell Buckle, is a lifetime dream for owners Judith Burgess and Larry Lowman. Designing a breeding farm where they could enjoy their passion for Tennessee Walking Horses was a dream come true. Together they have owned and shown an astonishing number of World Champion winners and have built one of the premier farms in the industry. Bridlewood Farm gives organized tours and offers a unique look at the industry. Call in advance 931-389-9388.

KATI'S KROSS ROADS

Kati's Krossroads, 14 Railroad Sq. in Bell Buckle, is a unique Victorian-decorated, home furnishings boutique. You'll find Natures Own Potpourri made right in Bell Buckle, Spin Shades, Mary Millsaps Jewelry, florals, wreaths, lamps, handcrafted baskets, and the best selection of Christmas decorations. Check out Kati's new clothing line and accessories. Stop by this charming boutique Monday-Saturday 9 am-5 pm and Sunday noon-5 pm. Call 931-389-0180 or visit www.bellbuckletn.org.

The Cat's Meow

Little girls love to dress up! And for the little girl who loves her doll, why not give her a dress she'll treasure? Owners John and Lorinda Gambill offer a beautiful selection of handmade, matching dresses for girls and their 18-inch dolls. They also offer specialty hand lotions and personalized gifts.

The Cat's Meow, 25 Railroad Sq. in Bell Buckle, is open 10 am-5 pm Monday-Saturday. Call 931-389-0064 or visit www.catsmeowgifts.com online.

DISCOVER BRENTWOOD

Beautiful Brentwood is the 18th largest city in the State of Tennessee in resident population. It has some of the area's most beautiful homes. Much of the land that makes up Brentwood today was granted to Revolutionary War soldiers by the state of North Carolina during the 1700s. By the time of the Civil War, this little Middle Tennessee community had become one of the richest and most prosperous in the state, with its businesses and plantations flourishing. During the war, many of the beautiful old plantations were occupied by both the Union and Confederate soldiers. By the end of the war, most were in ruin. In the 1920s, Brentwood was "rediscovered" and many of the plantations were lovingly restored.

Historical Landmark

One of the town's greatest attractions is the historic Victorian farmhouse called Cool Springs House, which was built in the 1830s. This historic house was moved to Brentwood's Crockett Park, where it is now the focal point of the park's historic preservation area. It is available for weddings, receptions, commercial gatherings, and retreats.

Crockett Park is host to many exciting events throughout the year. The Nashville Symphony performs in the park as part of the summer concert series. There are numerous events held throughout the year in all of the city parks.

For more information about Brentwood, contact the Brentwood Chamber of Commerce at 615-373-1595 or visit www.brentwood.org online.

Brentwood
Fairs Festivals & Fun

April
>Easter Egg Hunt
>Arbor Day

May
>A Day In Brentwood's Past
>The Nashville Symphony

June
>International Dinner
>Library Foundation Garden and Pond Tour
>Concerts in Crockett Park

July
>July 4th Celebration
>Concerts in Crockett Park

October
>Brentwood Tour of Homes

December
>Christmas Tree Lighting
>Morning with Santa
>Brentwood Luminaries

❧ *Northgate Gallery,* Inc.,

1690 Mallory Ln. in Brentwood, is a family affair you do not want to miss. David Patterson, his daughter Mia Patterson Fleetwood, and her husband Jeff Fleetwood have been in the antique business for the past 48 years. But the family's love for fine furniture extends even further into the past with Mia's grandfather and great grandfather. Mia's grandfather was one of the very first importers of fine antiques after World War II, and her great grandfather traveled throughout middle Tennessee buying cherry corner cupboards and other pieces to take back to Chattanooga where he sold them to eagerly awaiting customers.

You, too, are sure to find something unique at Northgate. The gallery is a direct importer of antiques, as well as fine reproductions from England and France. With more than 20,000 square feet of showroom, it has a very large and diverse inventory. Customers, designers and collectors may select a single unique piece or enough pieces to furnish an entire home. The inventory is constantly changing with monthly arrivals from England and France, and because of Northgate's other 20,000-square-foot warehouse in Chattanooga, it maintains one of the largest inventories in the South.

In addition to the vast inventory, Northgate also offers the production of custom-made furniture from England and France. Using the finest cabinetmakers, Northgate can produce almost anything you request. Ask about Northgate's custom dining tables, conference tables, and partner desks.

Call 615-221-4341 or visit www.Northgateantiques.com or simply drop in and browse the huge and open showroom filled with lovely antiques. Business hours are from 9 am-6 pm Monday-Saturday. The showroom in closed on Sunday. *(Color photo featured in front section of book.)*

Brentwood Interiors

Expanding from a downtown Nashville location, Brentwood Interiors at 144 Wilson Pike first opened its doors in 1997. This family-owned-and-operated business, formerly known as The Salvage Store, has been selling home decorating items for more than 50 years. You'll find oriental rugs, fabrics, trims, drapery patterns and hardware, furniture, and artwork below retail prices. You'll also discover upholstery supplies, children's heirloom laces and fabrics, and fine tapestries at discount  prices. Shop Monday-Saturday 9 am-5 pm. Call 615-376-6361 or visit www.brentwoodinteriors.com online.

Hotels

Everyone recognizes the famous, trademark "slanted red roof" that means comfortable, quality lodging at economical prices. The Red Roof Inn in Brentwood is located at 8097 Moore's Ln. in the Cool Springs section of town close to great shopping, dining, and entertainment.

You'll consistently find high-quality rooms, friendly service, complimentary morning coffee, and your own copy of USA Today. The Business King rooms feature an enhanced work area with over-head lighting, modem dataport, speaker telephone and voice mail. You'll find an expanded cable line-up, movies, and video games available upon request.

Travelers love the fact that their children under 18 stay free, and pets (80 lbs. or less) are allowed—in the rooms. (Fido gives Red Roof Inn a "paws up!") There are 350 Red Roof locations nationwide, nine in Tennessee. For reservations or more information, call 800-RED-ROOF, 615-309-8860, or visit www.redroof.com online.

Jewelry

ELIZABETH GREGORY ⤳ FINE JEWELRY

The bright and brilliant displays of exquisite jewelry are breathtaking, and the owners are welcoming and respectful. Unlike many fine jewelry stores, Elizabeth Gregory Fine Jewelry is a comfortable and friendly place to shop, and you will love the personal attention from Gregory Meisch. The well-trained staff is extremely knowledgeable and helpful in assisting customers with selection or special jewelry design.

Elizabeth Gregory Fine Jewelry specializes in 18 karat white and yellow gold; platinum jewelry; gemstones; and diamonds. You'll love the creations from leading designers like Scott Kay, Christian Bauer, Charles Garnier, Paula Pate, and Barry Kronen; as well as items from Jewels by Star and Gem Platinum. The store, located in Brentwood at 214 Ward Cir., #900, is open Monday-Friday 10 am-5 pm and Saturday 11 am-4 pm. Call 615-370-5559.

Jerry Lindsey

Custom Jewelry

"You can't believe how many people ask me about this piece of jewelry because it's so unique and different!"

That's a comment owner Jerry Lindsey of Jerry Lindsey Custom Jewelry often hears from his customers.

A licensed gemologist and member of the Jewelers of America and the Tennessee Jewelry Association, this eight-time award-winning designer knows the joy of helping people create their dream piece. With more than 23 years experience in jewelry design, Jerry works with unusual gemstone cuts and 140 different types of gemstones in gold or platinum.

Jerry understands that when you're looking for the perfect piece of jewelry, you want something to fit your personality and lifestyle. Finding it among the shelves of mass-produced pieces at chain jewelry stores just isn't the answer. At Jerry Lindsey Custom Jewelry, you'll find one-of-a-kind pieces that reflect your personal style or the style of that special someone. You'll have the opportunity to choose from one of the custom-made pieces Jerry has already cre-

ated, or even take part in the design process. If you choose to have a new piece created, you'll enjoy sitting down with Jerry and sharing your likes and dislikes, not only in jewelry, but also in life, so that the final piece is as special as you are.

Jerry Lindsey Custom Jewelry, 5008 Thoroughbred Ln. in Brentwood, is open 10 am-6 pm Tuesday-Friday, 10 am-2 pm Saturday and Monday by appointment. For more information or an appointment, call 615-373-2902.

PUFFY MUFFIN

Standing beside her mother and grandmothers from a very early age, Lynda Stone began learning and loving the art of cooking, and began memorizing the recipes they so lovingly shared. Today, she shares her love for fine food and creative cooking with her own daughters, who came up with the catchy name for her wonderful restaurant—Puffy Muffin. Lynda began her business in 1986 at home when her children were young. She baked breads and rolls for local restaurants, as well as rented bakery space in grocery stores. Today, Lynda and her staff of 48 are ready to serve you at the Puffy Muffin, 229 Franklin Rd. in Brentwood.

Her vision and enthusiasm for the restaurant are gifts from the Lord, and her desire is to continue to follow His lead. "Our goal is to delight each customer with delicious food and attentive service, she says. "We try hard to lend a personal touch to everything we do here."

You'll love everything on the menu. For breakfast try the awesome omelets, delicious biscuits and gravy or potato casserole—and, of course, the best "muffins" you've ever tasted! For lunch, choose from fresh salads, homemade soups, or hunger-busting sandwiches. Entrées include Amaretto Chicken, Quiche, Crab Cakes and Crunchy Chicken Casserole. And, the dessert menu boasts such wonderful delights as Italian Cream, German Chocolate, Chocolate Ganaché, Caramel Cakes and Three-Layer Sour Cream Coconut Cakes. Stop by Monday-Friday, 7 am to 6 pm—lunch served 10:30 am to 2:30 pm. Open Saturday, 8 am to 5 pm—brunch served 8 am to 2:30 pm. For catering information, call 615-373-2741 or visit www.puffymuffin.com.

Hair Expressions

Patti Brown and her very talented staff of professionals have only one goal—to make every customer look and feel absolutely beautiful! Hair Expressions, 245 Franklin Rd., is Brentwood's largest full-service salon. With 22 hair stylists, six manicurists, and three estheticians, Hair Expressions offers the latest trends in hairstyling, skin care, and nail services. Hours are Monday-Saturday 8:30 am-6 pm. Call 615-373-2415.

DISCOVER CLARKSVILLE

Advertised as a town, "Where Rivers Roll, Spires Rise, and Eagles Soar," Clarksville is one of the South's most historic cities and Tennessee's fastest growing city, behind only Memphis and Nashville. It is both a place of rich heritage and a vibrant city on the move. The breathtaking scenery along the beautiful Cumberland River bluffs and rolling rural hills complement a bustling business and entertainment center with exciting and memorable options for visitors. Say the word "Clarksville" to most baby boomers, and they will immediately start singing the tune made famous by the Monkees during the 1970s. The L & N Train Station in Clarksville was built in 1890, and served as the scene for the Monkees' famous hit song, *Last Train to Clarksville*.

For the History Buff

Clarksville was founded in 1784 as a settlement along the banks of the Cumberland and Red Rivers by Revolutionary War hero John Montgomery. It became Tennessee's first incorporated city in 1785. Tobacco trade flourished in Clarksville throughout the early years, and you can still smell the nostalgic aroma of smoking tobacco barns along the winding country roads. One way to glimpse the early history of this beautiful area is to visit Historic Collinsville, a restored pioneer settlement featuring outbuildings that date from the 1830s to 1870. The Customs House Museum and Cultural Center is also a must for history buffs. It is Tennessee's second largest general history museum, as well as one of the region's most photographed buildings. Located in the heart of the historic downtown district, this museum highlights ever-changing historical exhibits and an "Explorer's Floor," great for the entire family. Explore Civil War history at Fort Donelson Battlefield, a beautifully preserved field of the North's first major victory, and Fort Defiance, a Civil War outpost overlooking the Cumberland and Red Rivers used by the Confederate Army.

Clarksville is also known for its meandering, signature river-front promenade known as the Cumberland Riverwalk. It is the centerpiece of the River District—a 15-acre park featuring a River Center with playgrounds, picnic areas, an amphitheater, and a pedestrian walk to the downtown area. During the year, it is host to outdoor festivals and the Concert in the Park Series.

Shop Till You Drop

Clarksville's historic downtown is a thriving business center filled with wonderful shopping opportunities, charming cafes and restaurants, art galleries, theaters, museums, and beautiful architecture. The restored brick sidewalks and intersections, period lighting, benches, and colorful planters are a beautiful backdrop for exciting adventures and fun-filled days.

Shoppers will find everything from small, tucked-away collectible shops and clothing boutiques to widely recognized anchor stores at Governor's Square Mall. Restaurants serve everything from fried catfish and pit-smoked barbecue to fine steak and gourmet cuisine.

Need for Speed?

Clarksville is also home to the *Screaming Eagles,* the 101st Airborne Division, America's only Air Assault division. The Don F. Pratt Memorial Museum, which is located at Fort Campbell, traces the history of the unit from World War II to Operation Desert Storm, and features aircraft, military equipment, and monuments that capture the imagination. If you are visiting during the summer, you'll have the opportunity to take part in "Week of the Eagles," featuring an air show, parachute and helicopter demonstrations, and fun children's events. Or . . . if you feel the "need for speed," the Clarksville Speedway Racing Complex will satisfy with drag races for street cars and motorcycles, and go-cart races for the young ones.

We encourage you to explore every part of Clarksville, to amble through the downtown river district, enjoy fine feasts, and get to know the friendly, charming locals who open their arms and doors to visitors with true Tennessee hospitality.

For more information about Clarksville, contact the Clarksville-Montgomery County Economic Development Council, Chamber of Commerce, or Convention and Visitors Bureau at www.clarksville.tn.us, or call 800-530-2487 or 931-551-4313

Clarksville
Fairs Festivals & Fun

January
North Tennessee Winter Open

March
Old Time Fiddlers'
Championship

April
Concerts in the Park (April-
October)
Gateway Motor Drags (April-
November)
Queen City Road Race
Clarksville Senior Games
Rivers & Spires Festival
Mid-South Jazz Festival
International Day
Clarksville Kennel Club Dog
Shows

May
Jazz on the Lawn (May-
October)

July
Independence Day Celebration
& Carnival
North Tennessee State Fair

September
Riverfest

October
Fall Festival
Oktoberfest
Fall Pilgrimage & Gospel Jubilee
Antique Tractor & Engine Show
Intertribal Pow-wow
Miss Tennessee USA & Miss
Tennessee Teen USA Pageants

November
Christmas on the Cumberland

December
Christmas on the Cumberland
Clarksville Trees of Christmas
Customs House Christmas

Antiques

THE LEGACY ANTIQUES

Bret Appleton appropriately named his wonderful antique emporium "The Legacy," hoping that every item he sells will someday be a family treasure. The Legacy Antiques, 2501 Hwy. 41A Bypass in Clarksville, is filled with wonderful antique glassware, china, crystal, furniture and  collectibles. You will love browsing through all the vignettes filled with antique books, estate jewelry, unique bed frames and armoires, and a wonderful selection of authentic antiques at very reasonable prices. The Legacy Antiques reflects the knowledge and expertise of Bret's niece and manager Tia Keese, Bret's cousin Glenda Clardy, and family friends Lonnie Patterson and Courtney Leudenburg to provide exceptional antiques to the people of Clarksville. Stop by Monday-Saturday 9 am-5 pm and Sunday 1-4 pm. You will be valued as a customer and considered a friend. To place an order or to learn more, call 931-551-3442.

Memory Makers

Donna Ely has a little of just about everything you'll want to make your house a comfortable, beautiful reflection of your personality and style. From home décor and accessories to jewelry and fine baby gifts, Memory Makers, 1923 Madison St. Ste. A in Clarksville, has got you covered!

You'll find unusual items like Vera Bradley purses and Americana items by David. Donna also carries beautiful sterling silver jewelry and a large selection of the Aromatique and Yankee Candles. Customers absolutely love the beautiful custom-made gift baskets, filled with unique treasures sure to brighten anyone's day.

Memory Makers, "Clarksville's Most Unique Shop," is open Monday-Friday 10 am-6 pm and Saturday until 5 pm. For more information, call 931-221-0030. Complimentary gift-wrap with every purchase!

Body, Mind & Spirit, Inc.

As a military wife, Annette Cunningham was exposed to many different cultures and religions throughout the world, and found comfort in stores that promoted inner beauty and spiritual wellness. When she opened Body, Mind & Spirit at 1987 Madison St. in Clarksville, she began helping others find "good for the soul" gifts, books, videos, relaxation music, aromatherapy products, jewelry, and crystals. The store is open Monday-Friday 9 am-7 pm and Saturday until 5 pm. Call 931-906-7267.

Simply Brigitte
Home & Garden Design

"Simply Brigitte Home and Garden Design," located at 1501 Madison St. in a beautifully restored 1940s gas station, is a true Clarksville treasure. Owners Brigitte and Russ Newman have created a unique European-style shop and nursery that elevates home and garden design to a new level. You'll find wonderful Shabby Chic furniture, birdhouses, custom European floral designs, fountains, and live bedding plants. Visit Monday-Saturday 9 am-5 pm. For more information, call 931-648-0444.

Imagine stylish designer and traditional apparel for women and children at 20-60 percent off retail. At Madison Avenue Boutique, 1923 Madison St. in Clarksville, you don't have to dream anymore. Let Valerie Daley and her friendly staff find the ideal outfit for you. Then, finish off your designer duds with awesome accessories—handbags, shoes, jewelry and more. Stop by Monday-Friday 10 am-6 pm and Saturday until 5 pm. Call 931-648-2424.

Famous Tennessean

Wilma Rudolph (1940-1994) — born in Clarksville, overcame Polio as a child, but went on to earn numerous Olympic medals in the 1956 and 1960 Olympics. On September 7, 1960, in Rome, Wilma became the first American woman to win three gold medals in the Olympics.

Jewelry

As a military wife who traveled and moved frequently over the years, Sylvia Moore never considered owning her own business. Until…she was diagnosed with breast cancer in 1998 and moved back to Clarksville to be near family. With a great health report and a renewed sense of purpose, Sylvia found the art of beading and says, "I haven't been the same since!" Her delightful and dazzling store, Busy Beads & Moore, is a fun, unique jewelry experience.

Creative artisans teach classes and are on staff daily, so you can create your own designs. Busy Beads & Moore, 1817-A Madison St. #5, specializes in parties for groups of all sizes and ages and is an authorized dealer for Zoppini Italian modular charm bracelets. The store is open Monday-Friday 10 am-5:30 pm and Saturday until 3 pm. For class information, call 931-552-5545 or visit www.busybeadsonline.com.

DISCOVER
CLIFTON/WAYNESBORO

CLIFTON

The natural beauty of the Tennessee River is a powerful draw to this growing Middle Tennessee town. Clifton was named because of its location—high on a cliff, overlooking the banks of the beautiful river. In fact, Main Street ends where the town began—at the riverbank.

Rich in History
Many Clifton residents can trace their ancestry back to King Prater, the first non-Indian child born in Wayne County. In the beginning, Clifton was called "Ninevah," but the name changed in 1840 when work began on the Clifton Turnpike. During the Civil War, while most of the surrounding areas were loyal to the Union, Clifton aligned itself with the Confederacy, and suffered untold damage during the skirmishes. In fact, the Union headquarters were located in what is now the front yard of the Frank Hughes School. It is believed that only four homes survived the Civil War carnage, and only one public building. That building, the Presbyterian Church, still stands today.

Clifton's "Golden Years" were those of the late 1800s and early 1900s when the steamboat was king. The port made the town a destination for new businesses and opportunities. The Roaring Twenties; however, ushered in the town's decline, which lasted through the 50s, 60s, and early 70s. It wasn't really until the early 1980s that Clifton began to see the beginning of a "rebirth," and experience the transformation into an up-and-coming city. Through the last 20 years, Clifton has seen an energized downtown district, new businesses, and the beginning of new projects, thrusting it forward as a destination city once again. A new city marina is under construction, which will include new boat slips, new fuel tanks, camping facilities, and restaurants. The city of Clifton also operates three beautiful parks, including the scenic overlook at the edge of town. This low stoned walled area and iron gate surround a memorial to the veterans killed in action. From this point, you'll also see the original ferry landing, which although quiet today, was once alive with gunboats, transports, mail boats, and trading vessels.

Outdoor Adventures

Just as the river was once an essential part of Clifton's survival, today it is a natural draw for tourists. It is the perfect place to relax and rejuvenate. From leisurely scenic hikes to outdoor recreation such as fishing and boating, the river beckons visitors to the area. There are many opportunities for families to "play together" in Clifton, including golfing, hunting, water skiing, bird watching, horseback riding, picnicking and biking.

As you can imagine, with the surrounding waterways as a natural provider of fresh seafood, it's on the menu here a lot! Riverside restaurants serve up the best fried catfish you'll ever taste, along with great down-home "country cuisine."

Shopping Extravaganza

Love to shop? Shopping opportunities include sweet country roadside antique stores, garden shops, and mom & pop cottages, as well as a downtown district lined with gift shops and an old-fashioned pharmacy. We hope you will enjoy visiting these wonderful businesses and getting to know the owners—you'll get a true sense of small town hospitality!

WAYNESBORO

From camp meetings and trail rides to fireworks shows and parades, Waynesboro, Tennessee is a town that loves to celebrate. The locals will seize any occasion to bring out the guitars, fiddles, and banjos, and pack up the fried chicken and potato salad. One of the most exciting festivals each year is "Mad Anthony Wayne Day," usually held in June. Music, music, music, arts and crafts, antique car and tractor shows, "Tour de Wayne" bicycle ride, games and prizes, and lots of delicious food!

And Now For Something Really Different

The town and county were named for General Anthony Wayne, a Revolutionary War hero who fought alongside George Washington. He was one of the most colorful commanders ever to serve in the United States Army, which is why he was dubbed "Mad Anthony." General Wayne was regarded as a military genius during his day, but his greatness as an organizer of troops is only now beginning to be recognized. He was fierce in leadership and fierce in his dedication to country, evidenced by his famous words to George Washington during the war, "Issue the order sir, and I will storm hell!"

Waynesboro is also known throughout Middle Tennessee as a hunter's paradise. Sportsmen come from across the state to hunt, fish, and camp on more than 10,000 acres of privately owned and managed land. Rent a canoe and spend a glorious day on the beautiful Buffalo River. Then, end your day by finding a cozy country cabin to rest your weary bones.

Great Places, Great People

Of course, we came here to find the best shopping, dining, and family entertainment opportunities, and we found those, too. From antique stores and craft markets to restaurants owned by "great cooks," we discovered great places and people you will love getting to know.

For more information about Clifton, contact the Clifton Area Chamber of Commerce at 931-676-6966 or visit www.cliftonchamber.com online. Or, contact the Clifton Tennessee City Hall at 931-676-3370 or visit www.cityofclifton.com online.

For information about Waynesboro, contact the Wayne County Chamber of Commerce at 931-722-9022, or visit www.waynecountychamber.org online.

Clifton/Waynesboro Fairs Festivals & Fun

April
> Easter Egg Hunt

June
> Mad Anthony Wayne Day

July
> Fireworks Show
> Fourth of July in the Park

September
> Horseshoe Bend Festival

October
> Pumpkin Harvest Festival

December
> Christmas Parade

Eva Ruth & Co.

Eva Ruth Warren has her very busy and very talented hands in several businesses here in Clifton. Locals may know her as the city's Vice-Mayor, but visitors will remember her as the owner of River's Edge Stained Glass at 113 Main St. Stop by Monday-Thursday 10 am-5 pm, Friday until 3 pm, and Saturday until 2 pm or, call 931-676-5545. She and her husband Donny can also help you with landscaping needs, backhoe services, hauling of gravel and rock, storage and hardware. Call 931-676-5279.

River's Edge
Stained Glass

Gifts & Home Décor

Cousins

The staff is used to it by now—first-time customers begin to "ooh and aah" the minute they walk through the door of Cousins. This incredibly beautiful store will take your breath away. It is in a class by itself, and words cannot do justice to its charm. Cousins is located at 102 Public Sq. W. in Waynesboro, in two buildings that the owner's father and grandfather built many years ago to serve as their law office. The gift store was the dream of two Wayne County teachers—"cousins." But, shortly after its opening, tragic family circumstances necessitated one cousin leaving the venture. Ann Bevis continues the dream for the two with Cousins—a home décor and gift store unrivaled in this part of Tennessee.

The shop has two floors with various sections and individual rooms luxuriously decorated in different colors and themes. On the main floor, you'll find an array of unique gift items for women, including Aromatique bath and body products, Lux candles, beautiful handbags, and exquisite jewelry. A "teen room" sports the front and back of a '56 Chevy, and lots of fun, very hip gifts and cosmetics. The second floor has four rooms. The "bride's room" displays china, crystal, cut glass pieces, silver and wedding accessories. A "pink and blue room" is filled with cuddly baby gifts and clothing (0-24 months,) and a brightly-colored room is jampacked with wonderful children's gifts. Last, but definitely not least, there's a "Tennessee Room" or "heaven" for die-hard University of Tennessee fans!

You will absolutely love every minute of your visit. Ann and her staff are extremely friendly and helpful, and the store is a true sensory delight. Cousins is open Tuesday-Friday 10 am-5 pm and Saturday 10 am-4 pm. Contact Ann at 931-722-9947.

WILLOUGHBY DRUGS

Think "Mayberry," and you'll have a picture of this quaint, beautiful little Clifton drugstore and gift shop at 104 Main St. You'll find a large selection of greeting cards, Trapp Candles and much more. Another treat? The view from the front window is a breathtaking two-mile stretch of the beautiful Tennessee River! Open Monday-Friday 9 am-6 pm, only until 4 pm on Wednesday and Saturday until noon. For more information, call 931-676-3318.

Museums

T. S. STRIBLING MUSEUM & LIBRARY

A visit to the T.S. Stribling Museum & Library at 300 E. Water St. will give you an insight into some of Clifton's most illustrious ancestors, all with a "Story to Tell!" The T.S. Stribling House was renovated through a grant from the Tennessee Valley Authority, and it's open to the public for tours. The tour will feature information on Mr. Stribling, whose book "The Store" won a Pulitzer Prize in the 1930s; riverboat captain Charles Beard; and several confederate soldiers of the era. The museum is open Tuesday-Friday 11:30 am-6:30 pm. To learn more, call 931-676-3678 or visit www.cityofclifton.com online.

RIVERSTONE ESTATES

The view from your front porch could be of the Delta Queen Steamboat gliding by or a rolling hillside sloping into a white sandbar. Whether you enjoy fishing, boating, golfing, or just incredible river views, you'll find the perfect property at Riverstone Estates. Located at Bath Springs in the hillside along the Tennessee River, Riverstone is only four miles from Clifton. It is a 152-acre gated and restricted community where homeowners benefit from the splendor of country living without sacrificing the convenience to major metropolitan areas. It is only five miles from Bear Trace Golf Course, an 18-hole course designed by Jack Nicklaus. And, there is a new marina with 30 foot, 50 foot, and 60 foot boat slips, a fuel dock, and two boat ramps. You can choose from waterfront or water view lots on the Tennessee River, which provides wonderful fishing, boating, and water skiing opportunities during the summer. With its low utility and tax rates, very temperate climate, and low crime rate, Riverstone Estates is an ideal place to live or retire. In fact, this area has been rated as one of the top 10 places to retire in the United States. The office is located in Savannah at 9220 Hwy. 128 and is open Monday-Friday 7 am-5 pm. Call 731-925-1893 to speak with an agent or visit online to enjoy a picture gallery of available properties at www.tnriverproperties.com.

United Country· Riverbend Realty

Selling the South one piece at a time, United Country Riverbend Realty, 124 Main St., specializes in farms, hunting land, waterfront, and private getaways. David Pittard and Tommy Styers invite you to come to Clifton, their sleepy little river town located on the high bluffs of the Tennessee

River. Clifton is one of Tennessee's best-kept secrets. Call 931-676-3246 or visit www.unitedcountry.com/cliftontn/.

3 F 17

FORREST'S RAID
—— Dec. 15. 1862 ——

At Clifton, 8 mi. N., Forrest crossed, the river with 1800 cavalrymen and 4 guns, on a 200 mile raid into west Tennessee. Recrossing there on Jan. 1,1863, he had torn up three trunk railroads: taken more Federal prisoners than he had soldiers, taken or destroyed ten guns and military stores worth millions. He had immobilized more than ten times his strength in Federal troops, delaying Grant's Vicksburg campaign for 6 months.

TENNESSEE HISTORICAL COMMISSION

The Pirate's Lair

Son of a gun, gonna have big fun on the bayou! Clifton has a little bit of a Cajun accent here at The Pirate's Lair, 106 Main St. The gift shop was opened in 1998, and then the restaurant was added in 1999. Choose from crab legs, crawfish, shrimp, and fresh-shucked oysters, as well as red beans and rice, Creole, jambalya, seafood gumbo, and etouffee. The Pirate's Lair is open Friday and Saturday nights from 5-10 pm. Enjoy live musical entertainment year round. Call 931-676-6972.

Staff of Life

Dining at Staff of Life is more than just enjoying delicious dishes that happen to be good for you. You will be nourished with food for thought as well. Owner Carlyn Wilson is recognized as one of the foremost authorities on diet, nutrition and health issues, and she has been working in these fields for more than 20 years. When she opened Staff of Life at 198 Crossno Cemetery Rd., it was with a desire to help others with questions about their personal health, provide confidential consultations about lifestyle changes, and teach her customers about the virtues of healthy cooking.

Staff of Life is tucked into the beautiful rural countryside of Clifton, and though it may be a little hard to find, it is definitely worth the adventure. You will enjoy wonderful dishes such as Polenta with Mushrooms and Grilled Veggies, Eggplant Parmesan, and Rosemary and Cheese Stuffed Ravioli with Butternut Spinach. Enjoy chicken and seafood dishes, wonderful vegetables, and delicious desserts. In fact, the restaurant is known for its Tofu New York Cheese Cake and Ice Cream, made without sugar, eggs, milk, or animal products.

Carlyn has presented demonstrations from coast-to-coast and been extensively published on her knowledge of raw foods and food combinations. She offers free cooking classes at the restaurant, which fill up quickly, so be sure to call soon. She is available for cooking schools and seminars throughout Tennessee, and her videotapes are

available, featuring recipes from her cookbooks. The restaurant is open Tuesday through Friday 11:30 am-3:30 pm, Tuesday and Thursday evenings 6-9 pm and Sunday 1-6 pm. Visit www.bibleschoolofhealth.com online or call 931-676-3503 for directions.

Tennessee Fitness *Spa*

Historic Natural Bridge, just 95 miles southwest of Nashville, is the only known double-span natural bridge formation in the world, bordered by the crystal clear waters of the Forty-Eight Creek. Natural Bridge is the location for the incredible Tennessee Fitness Spa, a fitness and weight loss destination. Guests of all ages travel from around the world to enjoy a healthy, invigorating experience at one of Tennessee's most beautiful sites. The spa, 299 Natural Bridge Park Rd., 10 miles outside of Waynesboro, focuses on weight loss, fitness education, and de-stressing. The program is based on nutrition and exercise, and the staff is friendly, helpful and very nurturing.

You may choose from a variety of weekly programs (or shorter stays if available) at very reasonable prices. Days begin with a delicious, healthy breakfast and a two to 10 mile walk through the beautiful countryside. Daily activities include aerobics, circuit training, aquacise, toning, yoga or stetching classes, and more. After dinner, you can take part in "movie night," bingo, arts and crafts, special entertainment, or educational lectures. Optional services include facials, manicures, pedicures, body wraps, hair styling, and massage therapy. You can also take advantage of their 30 foot by 60 foot heated swimming pool, 10-person hot tub, sauna, 5,000 square foot gym, and racquetball court.

The rustic, chalet-style accommodations are clean and comfortable, featuring large porches for relaxing, with daily housekeeping service. The rates include a full schedule of fitness activities and three healthy meals a day. Office hours are Monday-Friday 8 am-5 pm, Saturday 8 am-noon and Sunday 9 am-5 pm. For more information, call 800-235-8365, 931-722-5589 or visit www.tfspa.com online.

DISCOVER
COOKEVILLE / CROSSVILLE /
MURFREESBORO

COOKEVILLE

If you want to escape the hustle and bustle of the big city and enjoy the slow, quaint, small-town atmosphere, you'll find it here in Cookeville. The town was founded in 1855 and named for one of the area's most prominent citizens of the antebellum period—Major Richard Cooke. If you stroll the sidewalks of Dixie Avenue, you'll see houses dating to the 1900s, which were established by the early settlers who founded Dixie College (now Tennessee Tech University). A tour through Cookeville's historic residential district from Freeze Street to East Seventh Street is a collection of 20th Century architecture, including Queen Anne, Neo-Classical, Colonial Revival, Tudor Revival, and Bungalow.

Downtown Charm

The Historic Westside area is a delightful combination of specialty shops, restaurants, antique stores, and pubs—all within walking distance to the Cookeville Depot Museum. The Cookeville Depot Museum was built in 1909 by the Tennessee Central Railroad and is listed on the National Register of Historic Places. Surrounded by a beautiful park, the Depot displays railway artifacts, old photos of the early days of the railroad era in Putnam County, a running scale train, and two touring cabooses.

Cookeville's downtown historic Courthouse Square, which is

in the midst of a full-swing preservation program, is filled with a variety of unique stores, coffeehouses, and galleries. While on the square, be sure to visit the Arcade Building to see the beautiful stained glass panels on the ceiling of what was the first enclosed shopping mall of its kind in Cookeville. Shop till you drop, or spend your time here outdoors discovering the wonderful beauty of the area at Cane Creek Park. The park offers boating, biking, hiking, fishing, basketball, volleyball, and great picnicking areas. There's never a dull moment in this fun, little town. Exciting festivals and special events are scheduled throughout the year, including: Railroad Rendezvous Springfest, Freedom Fest, the U.C. Quilt Festival, Middle Tennessee Antique Engine & Tractor Show, Cookin' on the Square, and the traditional Christmas Parade. Cookeville is definitely, "A Main Street Community, Where Southern Hospitality is On Track Year Round!"

CROSSVILLE

The "salt-of-the-earth" folks of Crossville, Tennessee, are one of the town's most impressive attributes, but nature does a pretty good job at vying for your attention, as well. Visitors are in awe of the beautiful valleys, mountains, plateaus, rivers, creeks, and lakes of this Cumberland Plateau city. Prior to 1805, the entire Cumberland County was Indian Territory, with arrowheads and relics carbon dated to be thousands of years old. In 1797, Francis Bailey wrote of the area, "It is a fine large plain or natural meadow containing many hundreds of acres and covered throughout its whole extent with a tall rich grass surrounded on every side by the neighboring mountains and watered with several fine springs which flow from one end to the other."

How It All Began

Crossville was first called Lambeth's Cross Roads because several important roads crossed at this point. However, the name was changed to Crossville by the end of the 1800s. When the town was incorporated in 1901, it had a hotel, a bank, a railroad and a depot, and several stores. Today it is called "The Golf Capital of

Tennessee," and it is a destination location for wonderful hunting, fishing, boating, hiking, and absolutely great "bargain hunting!"

One of the best ways to experience the history of Crossville and the surrounding Cumberland Plateau is to visit the Cumberland Homesteads, just four miles south of the city on Hwy. 127. This "community" began during the early 1930s as a homesteading project, and much of the natural rural countryside beauty has remained unchanged. The Homesteads were built during the Depression under the Franklin D. Roosevelt administration to help "economically stranded" families of farmers, miners, and timber workers who had lost their jobs. Each "homestead" was furnished with all of the tools for self-sufficiency, including farm animals and tools essential for farm life. The Homestead Tower and Museum on Hwy. 68 depicts the story of this Depression Era program, as well as providing a wonderful insight to the first homestead families. The octagonal stone tower is a marvel of innovative design itself. It houses a water tank and a winding stairway leading to the platform lookout. There, you can see most of the original 252 farmsteads. Four rooms at the base are used for museum displays and exhibits, which include photos, documents, and artifacts. You will learn that although many of the original families have moved, a sizeable number have remained, becoming an integral part of the history and culture of Crossville and Cumberland County.

Another beautifully preserved part of Crossville-Cumberland history can be found at the historic "Grassy Cove" on Hwy. 68. It is one of the most remarkable, geologically unique valleys in the Southeast, and includes the well-known Salt Petre Cave. Grassy Cove has been carefully preserved by the descendants of the white settlers who arrived here in the early 1800s. Take a guided tour of the Cove, which highlights historical sites like the J.C. Kemmer & Son General Store, The Grassy Cove United Methodist Church and Cemetery, and the Grassy Cove Academy. History buffs will love it!

Tee Time

Or, if you're more of the outdoorsy type, grab your clubs and head for the beautiful courses in Cumberland County. Golf has emerged as one of Crossville and Cumberland County's major attractions. In fact, Crossville has more golf holes per person than any other place in Tennessee. Whether you are a complete amateur (or "duffer"), or a seasoned professional, there is something for everyone. Eleven beautiful courses include three that were named in the "Top 10 Places to Play in Tennessee"—Renegade Mountain, Heatherhurst and Stonehenge. Each course is unique, offering a different experience. Breathtaking, postcard vistas, rolling hills, crystal-clear streams, and pure mountain air make the courses as beautiful as they are challenging.

A Lady's Day Out On The Town

Crossville is one of the South's best kept secrets. With its rolling valleys, towering forests, and crystal-clear waters, it is the perfect place to "get away from it all," and a wonderful place to explore a quaint downtown area, filled with interesting and exciting adventures. Be sure to visit the historic Palace Theatre, which re-opened in 2001 as a Community Auditorium and Information Center. Also, a must see, the Crossville Depot, which was built in 1900 and served as the famous scene from the movie "Sgt. York" starring Gary Cooper, as well as the Cumberland General Store, an old-time store featuring items for the country kitchen. Don't miss the Cumberland County Playhouse, a nationally recognized theatre that features Broadway and local productions; and many wonderful shops that personify the warmth and friendliness that is Crossville. Just outside the city, high atop the Plateau, you'll find the Stonehaus Winery, the county's first licensed winery in the 20th Century. Pack a picnic and enjoy the serenity of Tennessee's beautiful plateau.

We know that you will find Crossville to be "Everything You've Been Looking 'Fore!'" From delightful boutiques and specialty shops; quaint, cozy eateries, and bargain factory outlets to world-class golf and exciting recreational activities, take time to enjoy the smiling faces and neighborly ways of Crossville! For information on guided tours or customized itineraries, contact Martha Hale ETC Tours at 931-484-0207. Martha will ensure that you experience The Cumberlands of Tennessee with a knowledgeable and experienced guide.

MURFREESBORO

Visitors to Murfreesboro are often surprised at the many exciting activities and adventures offered in this town. Whether your passion is Civil War history, antebellum mansions or, of course, wonderful shopping, you'll love the time spent in this charming town.

Savor the History

Murfreesboro was named in 1811 for Revolutionary War Hero Colonel Hardy Murfree. It's no wonder it's the county seat for Rutherford County. Civil War buffs will love hanging out downtown. The beautiful Rutherford County Courthouse on the town's public square is one of only six remaining Tennessee courthouses built before the Civil War, and is listed on the National Register of Historic Places. It was a strategic building during the war, occupied by both Confederate and Union soldiers.

One of the most interesting adventures in Murfreesboro will be your visit to Cannonsburgh, a pioneer village constructed in 1974 as an American Revolution Bicentennial project. This replica of a rural Southern village is a delightful journey back in time, covering 125 years of Southern life in Tennessee from 1800-1925. There is a grist mill, a one-room schoolhouse, an early 1800s Town Hall, a doctor's office, a blacksmith shop, and a general store, a 1900s telephone building, a Civil War diorama, the L & N R.R. caboose, an American Frontier Covered Wagon, and the world's largest red cedar bucket! A treat for the entire family!

History buffs will also love their visit to the Stones River National Battlefield on the Old Nashville Highway. Here you can tour the battlefield and stand "in the slaughter pen" where Confederates captured Union artillery. You will see fields where cotton grew and cannons roared "so ear-shattering that soldiers paused to stuff their ears with cotton." And, you can stroll through one of the nations oldest National Cemeteries and reflect on the incredible sacrifice made by the 6,000 soldiers buried there.

A walking tour of Murfreesboro's Main Street will give you an idea as to the town's unique architecture and identity, and you will learn the history and strength of this town and all it has survived during the years. Don't miss Oaklands Historic House Museum—an antebellum home where Confederate President Jefferson stayed while in Murfreesboro.

We think that we have found some of the most wonderful treasures Murfreesboro has to offer, from the cozy antique stores and specialty boutiques to quaint and memorable eateries. Take time to enjoy this town's unique charm.

For more information about Cookeville, contact the Cookeville Area-Putnam County Chamber of Commerce at 800-264-5541, 931-526-2211 or visit www.cookevillechamber.com online. Or, contact the Upper Cumberland Tourism Association at 931-520-1088 or visit www.uppercumberland.org/ online.

For more information about Crossville, contact the Crossville Chamber of Commerce at 931-484-8444 or visit www.crossville.com online.

For more information about Murfreesboro, contact the Rutherford County Tennessee Chamber at www.rutherfordchamber.org online or call 800-716-7560, 615-893-6565. Or, contact the City of Murfreesboro at 615-893-5210 or visit www.murfreesborotn.gov online.

Cookeville Fairs Festivals & Fun

January
Magic Moments Bridal Show

February
MTAETA Swap Meet
Mardi Gras Masquerade Ball

March
Home Show

April
Breakfast with the Easter
Bunny
Lion's Club Walking Horse
Show
Dogwood Fridays – Concerts
in the Park
Window on the World
International Festival

May
Railroad Rendezvous
Springfest
CityScape's Taste of the Town

June
Sundays in the Park Concert
Series

July
Freedom Fest
TN Jr. Livestock Sheep
Exposition

August
Putnam County Agricultural &
Industrial Fair

September
Monterey Labor Day
Celebration
Fall Fun Fest
Tennessee State Championship
Cook-off
Stations of Imagination
U.C. Women's Show of
Cookeville
Middle Tennessee Antique
Engine & Tractor Show

October
Brown Bag Lunch Concerts
Standing Stone Celebration
Excursion Train-Cookeville to
Watertown
U.C. Quilt Festival
Enchanted Kingdom
Cookin' on the Square

November
Mistletoe Market
Santa's Workshop
Hidden Hollow Christmas
Lights
Christmas Parade

Crossville
Fairs Festivals & Fun

March
> Ms. Tennessee Senior America Pageant
> Home Show

April
> Easter Egg Hunt
> Gospel Fest
> Upper Cumberland District Senior Games
> Crossroads Arts and Craft Show
> Spring Flower and Garden Show

May
> Upper Cumberland District Senior Games
> Craft Fair on the Plateau
> Relay for Life

June
> Depot Days – A Main Street Festival
> Fly In at Crossville Municipal Airport

July
> Fireworks Festival
> Rodeo

August
> 127 Corridor Sale
> The Cumberland County Fair

October
> Pioneer Day on the Mountain
> Oktoberfest

December
> Christmas Parade
> Parade of Christmas Trees

Murfreesboro
Fairs Festivals & Fun

March
Tennessee Beef Agribition

April
Charlie Daniels Rodeo
Cannonsburgh Pioneer Day

May
Main Street Jazz Fest
Free Day in May

June
Secret Garden Tour
Juneteenth Celebration

July
Uncle Dave Macon Days Festival
Civil War Encampment
Antique Show & Sale

August
International Grand Championship Walking Horse Show

September
Pioneer Power Days
Old Timers' Day

October
Heritage Days
Heritage Festival

November
A Civil War Christmas

December
Heritage Christmas Tour of Homes
Oaklands Candlelight Tour of Homes
Bethlehem Marketplace

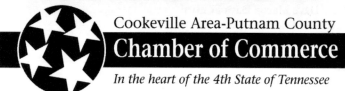

Cookeville Area-Putnam County
Chamber of Commerce
In the heart of the 4th State of Tennessee

If you love the charm and convenience of spending a day in a quaint downtown, visit a city recognized nationally for bringing vitality back to its main streets—Cookeville, Tenn. By taking a few dozen steps around Cookeville's revitalized downtown area, you can shop for antiques, browse unique stores, sample world and local cuisine, and visit the historic downtown Cookeville Depot Museum. Choose from a café featuring foods from around the world, fine Cajun dining, a popular local pub or a kitchen offering a variety of homemade soups. Round out your day with a visit to the nearby Appalachian Center for crafts or take a short hike to a 130-foot thunderous waterfall. For details on a day out in Cookeville or Putnam County, visit www.cookevillechamber.com online or call 800-264-5541, 931-526-2211.

Artists, Art Galleries, Gifts & Home Décor

Cumberland Art & Gift GALLERY

Cary Bowling says, "It's not just the thought . . . the gift matters too. So give a thoughtful gift!" Having traveled and worked in 25 states over a 15-year-period, Cary acquired quite an eye for unique gifts with "local flavor."

In Cumberland Art & Gift Gallery, 1740 Peavine Rd. (take exit #322 off I-40) in Crossville, Cary features the works of many of Tennessee's top craftsmen. You'll find pottery, copper garden items, hummingbird feeders, wooden bowls and spoons, cutting boards, cheese boards, gourds, baskets, soaps, candles, coffees, and homemade jams. They also have the best selection of turquoise jewelry in the area. A great idea? Take home a Tennessee Buddy Basket for someone special. You pick and choose the items, scents and flavors your friend will enjoy, and then have them wrapped in a unique basket. Open Tuesday-Friday 9 am-5 pm and Saturday 10 am-4 pm. Call 931-484-2939 or 877-304-0562.

Jenny Jackson Spurlock feels that she has been given a wonderful gift. She has the opportunity to honor her beloved mother every day in the beautiful store they built together—JJ Jax. Jenny and her mother Janice Jackson had always dreamed of owning a gift and floral boutique—a place where friends and visitors could shop, relax, and really enjoy themselves. When the historic 100-year-old home at 146 S. Lowe Ave. became available, everything just "fell into place," and JJ Jax became an instant success with the people of Cookeville. Jenny and Janice worked hard to make their dream come true, turning the house into a beautiful treasure trove of wonderful gifts for the home, garden, and office. The best part of the experience for Jenny was being able to work side-by-side with her wonderful mother. Sadly, Janice passed away suddenly in 1999, leaving a wonderful legacy, and memories that will inspire Jenny for a lifetime. In carrying out her mother's dream, Jenny has continued to delight customers with the ever-changing, eclectic displays of glassware, pillows, bath and body products, and wonderful ladies' accessories. She carries the largest selection of the popular Aromatique in the area, and has been designated as a "Brighton Heart Store"—an honor given to less than 5 percent of the Brighton retailers nationwide. You'll find the entire product line of Brighton products including handbags, belts, shoes, jewelry, wallets, key fobs, watches, sunglasses, fragrance, luggage, and other accessories. You will love the warm, friendly, and very colorful ambiance of JJ Jax. Enjoy a cup of gourmet coffee and homemade cookies while you shop, and discover a new friend in Jenny.

The shop is open from 9:30 am to 5 pm Monday–Saturday. For more information, call 931-526-6130.

Crossville Depot Gifts

As you browse through the wonderful array of tea, tea accessories, "girlfriend gifts," fun jewelry and scented candles, be sure to sample the "eye-rolling good" pecan honey jelly, fruited lemonade and teas, Tennessee tipsy coffee, or any of the assorted butters and fruit spreads. The Crossville Depot is the historic site on which WWI Hero Sgt. Alvin York returned to a hero's welcome, as depicted in the movie "Sgt. York" starring Gary Cooper. Located in downtown Crossville, 14 North St. Open 9 am-6 pm Monday-Saturday. Call 931-456-2586.

THE MARKET PLACE

Welcome to one of the most special treasures in Cookeville! The Market Place, 1166 S. Jefferson Ave., is a treat to the senses from the moment you walk through the doors of this beautiful two-story Southern house. It is a luxurious world of exquisite antiques, fine bed and bath linens, inspired scents and body products, sparkling hand-cut crystal, classic silver jewelry, unique accessories for the home, and delicious gourmet food treats. Shoe fanatics will also love this store! You'll find products from Peacock Alley, Lady Primrose, Trapp, Vietri, and Bentley Arbuckle. The Market Place is open Monday-Friday 9:30 am to 5 pm and Saturday 10 am to 4 pm. Call 931-526-GIFT (4438) or visit www.themrktplace.com to view the beautiful displays.

Cumberland County
Playhouse

Cumberland County Playhouse, one of the top 10 theaters in rural America, is a non-profit, professional theater established in 1965 by Broadway and Hollywood actor/writer/producer Paul Crabtree and the people of Cumberland County and Crossville. Most weeks of the year, there are three different shows playing.

Located on the high, windswept tableland of the mountains of Tennessee, the Cumberland Plateau at 221 Tennessee Ave., Cumberland County Playhouse draws people from across America. They produce Broadway style musicals and plays with Broadway talent, Juilliard students, seasoned professional actors from all over the country, and their own homegrown students from their nationally famous Dance and Theater Education Program. In the spring of 2003, they were one of only four theaters in the nation chosen to produce Cats for the first time in regional theater. (Cats returns in 2005.)

In 2004, by invitation of the Rodgers and Hammerstein organization in New York, the Playhouse will present the first American Premiere of a new version of "Two by Two," the last score composed by the great Richard Rodgers. The Playhouse is also the first theater in the world licensed by Disney to mount their classic musical, "Beauty and the Beast," independently!

Ticket prices are among the lowest in the nation for professional theater. Stop by! The playhouse is only two hours from Nashville; one hour from Knoxville; and one-and-a-half hours from Chattanooga. For tickets, call the Box Office at 931-484-5000 or email info@ccplayhouse.com online. Contact Jim Crabtree, Producing Director; Janet Kluender, Business Manager; or Miller Leonard, Creative Director of Marketing for more information. A trip to Tennessee is never complete without a visit to the nationally famous Cumberland County Playhouse. *(Color photo featured in front section of book.)*

Bed & Breakfasts, Cabins & Inns

For the special event in your lives, or just much-needed solitude and relaxation, we've found the absolute perfect place! Carriage Lane Inn, 411 Maney Ave., is one of the most quaint and charming bed and breakfast inns you will ever visit. The main house was built in 1899, and the street was the "carriage lane" to the Maney family home, which is now the Oakland Historic House Museum. Through the Civil War and post years, this little historic home saw a lot of neglect and abuse, but was lovingly rescued and renovated by the present owners, Ted and Sharon Petty. They purchased the two adjacent homes as well, which have been renovated as an inn and reception house.

The four-bedroom inn and three-bedroom cottage have uncluttered rooms, fireplaces, queen featherbeds, private baths, whirlpools, Cable TV/VCR, cordless phones, wireless internet service, and an office center. Guests will enjoy a complimentary snack bar and private breakfast in the rooms, porches, or gardens. Guests are walking distance from downtown Murfreesboro for shopping, dining, or entertainment, and a carriage is available on Friday and Saturday nights to tour the downtown streets. Bike or walk the greenway trails, wade in the creek, and picnic along the way. Kids will love the "hands-on" children's museum and pioneer village, all within walking distance from the inn.

For weddings, receptions, or private dinners, the reception house is a beautiful location. Carriage Lane Inn also features a secret garden surrounded by mature trees and a lovely border of flowers. For information or reservations, call 615-890-3630 or 800-357-2827 or visit www.carriagelaneinn.com.

McCoy Place
bed & breakfast

The best word we can find to describe this wonderful Crossville bed & breakfast is "idyllic." McCoy Place, 525 Roy McCoy Rd., is nestled in the middle of the 79,000-acre Catoosa Wildlife Reserve, and is surrounded by 100-year-old towering oaks, lush flower gardens, and fruit orchards. It is the family homeplace of owner Annette Hendrixson. The inn features many private areas and porches on which to read, relax, or nap—a place of quiet solitude, yet only a short drive to many area attractions and restaurants. You will enjoy a full gour-

met breakfast, refreshments in the afternoon, and turn-down service in the evenings. Open Thursday through Saturday, during April-October. Visit www.mccoyplace.com for a visual tour of the inn, or call 931-484-1243 for more information. Absolutely wonderful!

THE LUCKY STARR

Nestled in the breathtaking Sequatchie Valley in Pikeville at 5746 Upper E. Valley Rd., The Lucky Starr offers a rustic, cozy retreat in some of the most beautiful country imaginable. Choose between the larger two-story or the smaller cozy cabin—both have a fireplace, antique

furnishings, and lots of charm! The cabins back right up to the scenic four-acre Echo Lake, so canoe or fish to your heart's content. Contact owners Starr and Parky at 423-533-2100 or visit www.Luckystarr.com.

DeHoff
Christian Bookstore

This family-run Christian bookstore, church supply house, and publishing company, at 749 N.W. Broad St. in Murfreesboro, was founded in 1939 by Dr. George W. DeHoff, and specializes in Golden Rule Service. You will find 400 Bibles in several languages, children's books, VBS supplies, gift books, commentaries, and gold stamping on-site. Open Monday-Friday 9 am-5 pm and Saturday until 1 pm. Call 800-695-5385 or 615-893-8322 for a catalog by mail, or visit www.dehoffbooks.com.

Katherine's
Books & Collectibles

As you turn into the spacious parking lot at 5429 Peavine Rd., #102 in Crossville, you'll get a little taste of "Southern charm" at its best. Beautiful white wicker rocking chairs and cute café tables invite you to "sit awhile," and enjoy a wonderful book and a piece of homemade fudge! You absolutely will not be able to refrain—the smells drifting from the fudge kitchen are tantalizing. Katherine's is a fun store—a place filled with laughter, friends, and family—you'll love to visit time and again. Also, you will find a vast selection of collectibles from Beanie Babies and Disney to brass and bronze items. They also have a new line—Caren et Cie, a collection of lotions, gels, facial treatments, even laundry wash and home cleaners. A portion of profits from this line is donated to the Caren Singer Foundation for Breast Cancer Research. Open Monday-Saturday 9 am-6 pm and Sunday 1-6 pm. Call 931-456-2665 for more information.

When Cindy and Don Calcote moved to Cookeville they were excited to find a family-oriented, progressive community. After opening BookWorks, they became involved with a national program called City Scape, dedicated to the revitalization of downtown businesses. They took a big chance, moving BookWorks to one of the oldest buildings on the square at 230 E. Broad St. They renovated, added Poets on the Square, and turned the downstairs level into The Market on the Square. Although Book-Works and Poets were later sold to the present owners, they all work together to provide an incredible one-stop shopping experience! You will enjoy each one of these fabulous shops!

The Market on the Square, #6 N. Jefferson Ave., features everything from gourmet food and original artwork to jewelry. Stop by Monday-Saturday 9 am-9 pm and Sunday 1-6 pm, or call Cindy and Don at 931-372-7688.

BookWorks owner Judith Mariano, has two goals in mind, to be an uncommon bookstore specializing in finding "just the right" book for each customer and to create an atmosphere where everyone feels at home. Her handpicked, diverse selection of books and gift items compliment the trio. The children's room is full of books, art and stuffed critters guaranteed to delight the entire family. Open Monday-Saturday 9 am-11 pm and Sunday 1-6 pm. Call 931-372-8026.

Poets on the Square is a delightful, cozy place to sip a steaming cup of expresso, cappuccino, or gourmet coffee as you enjoy the works of the featured local artist. Coffee, breakfast, lunch, or dessert is served Monday-Saturday 7 am-11 pm and Sunday 1-6 pm. Contact owners Ted and Terri McWilliams at 931-372-2201 or www.poetscoffee.com online.

We found out why customers absolutely love this charming store. They adore the great selections of wonderful ladies' clothing and accessories, beautiful jewelry, great home décor, and the friendly, special attention from the owners. Robin's Boutique, 1459 Interstate Dr., Ste. B in Cookeville, was a dream come true for Robin Beckham. When her two boys were "out of the nest," she and her sister put their ideas and talents together to form this very special store. They carry great lines of easy-to-care-for, wrinkle-free clothing—perfect for businesswomen who travel—handbags, scarves, and fabulous jewelry. You can also make an appointment for airbrush tanning or cellulite body wraps. The store is open Monday-Friday 9 am to 6 pm and Saturday 10 am to 4 pm. For more information, call 931-520-7777.

Elite Repeats

Tracey Ruckersfeldt says, "Resale Beats Retail." We agree! She takes pride in presenting only the best quality in gently worn clothing and new accessories to her customers who have been "repeat" clients since 1994. Before Elite Repeats, Tracey was a personal shopper in Los Angeles for 10 years. Located at 151 Elmore St., in Crossville, you'll find the staff extremely friendly. Stop by Monday-Friday 10 am-5 pm and Saturday 9 am-3 pm. Contact Tracey at 931-484-8485.

Owners Dennis and Lois Wilbanks invite you to "shop till you drop" under shade trees, under sheds, or in the open at Tennessee's largest weekly Flea Market. The Crossville Flea Market, on Hwy. 70 N. between Knoxville and Nashville, still has a country fair atmosphere, with hundreds of booths and great concessions. Open every weekend and Memorial Day and Labor Day Mondays since 1976! Hours are 7 am-3 pm. Call 931-456-9674 or visit www.cross villefleamarket.com online.

TORI'S COTTAGE AND DESSERT CAFÉ

At only 5 years old, Tori Cannon became the owner of her own gift boutique in Crossville! Tori's Cottage and Dessert Café, 98 Interstate Dr., celebrates everything good in life; unusual gifts, gourmet coffee and extraordinary desserts. The store has seven rooms full of kitchen accessories, candles, gourmet foods, jewelry, stationery, Tori's own personal bath and body products and a room devoted to children. Tori was put in charge of the children's room and is responsible for selecting the merchandise for babies through teens. Tori says, "I get to sell the toys. That's the best part!" And sell she does! This tiny entrepreneur has a knack for knowing just "what will sell" from Hello Kitty to educational toys. Tori's was best described by a customer who said, "It's more than a gift shop, its an incredible shopping experience." And to top it off, in 2004 Tori's launched lunch featuring quiche and homemade soups to compliment the dessert café. Tori's mom, Sherrie Cannon, wants you to relax while shopping, sit back and eat some great food, talk with friends and enjoy your time in the Upper Cumberland. Open Monday-Saturday 9:30 am-5 pm. For more information call 931-707-8674.

When you want your gift to be as special as the person receiving it, trust Carol and John Bartlett and the talented staff at Abel Gardens to design the ultimate floral arrangement or gift basket. This popular floral and gift shop at 620 S. Jefferson Ave. #208 has been a favorite in Cookeville for more than 30 years. You'll find the most beautiful roses, tropicals and green plants, as well as exceptional gifts and home décor. Abel Gardens is an authorized dealer for "Old World Christmas" and carries a large selection of Demdaco Willow Tree Angels and collectibles by Pipka as well as Fitz and Floyd.

The shop is open Monday through Friday 8 am-6 pm and Saturday 9 am-2 pm. For more information, call 888-526-9797, 931-526-9797, or visit www.abelgardens.com online.

Debbie Gaw loves to have parties. In fact, "planning parties" is her business! Have A Party, 109 W. Broad St. offers same-day printing service on invitations and stationery. Debbie can help with everything from balloons to fabulous party favors. Whether you are giving a children's birthday party and need colorful bags filled with lots of fun favors, or a more grown-up event such as a graduation party, wedding reception, or corporate events, visit this wonderful store first. Customers also love the beautiful gift baskets Debbie creates for special occasions. Have a Party is located in Cookeville's Old Towne, just across from the historic Cookeville Depot Museum. Open Monday-Saturday 9 am-5 pm. Contact Debbie at 931-372-7595 for all of your party and delivery needs, and prove her motto, "We Deliver Smiles!"

Hotels

One of the newest and most impressive travel inns in the area is the business-and-family-friendly Baymont Inn & Suites, 1151 S. Jefferson Ave. The rooms include oversized desks, task lighting, and computer data ports. The hotel has just added wireless high-speed Internet access in all rooms as well as other areas of the property. Just think—finishing a day's work poolside would put a smile on any business traveler's face! Families love the large televisions, free cable, hair dryers, irons, and coffeemakers. A deluxe, hot continental breakfast that includes waffles or French toast is served each morning in the lobby, and the staff is extremely friendly and helpful. You won't be surprised to learn that this new Cookeville hotel took top honors as the 2003 President Award winner and the 2003 White Glove Award winner. Visit www.baymontinns.com/cookeville online or call 800-301-0300 or 931-525-6668.

Jewelry

Visit Shelton's at 155 W. Broad St., one block west of the Cookeville Depot Museum in historic downtown. Whether you are stopping in to select a breathtaking engagement ring, or simply have a watch battery replaced, you will receive very personal service. Shelton's, a Cookeville tradition since 1960, offers unique jewelry, home décor, and gift items. The store is open Monday-Friday 9:30 am-5:30 pm and Saturdays October-December. Call 931-526-2854 or visit www.sheltonsjewelry.com online.

MARINA'S ON THE SQUARE, INC.

As you stroll around historic downtown Murfreesboro and wander in and out of the lovely shops and stores, make sure you wander into Marina's on the Square and get a bite to eat. This quaint restaurant is as good if not better than any Old World, New York style Italian eatery. Customers say that Marina's has the best pizza in town and the best calzones you will eat anywhere. If you want something a little less casual, then try the chicken Marsala, baked salmon in lemon butter cream sauce, or the "not so spicy" Cajun chicken pasta. Be adventurous—all the food is absolutely delicious!

Marina's is considered the best Italian restaurant in Murfreesboro and is located at 125 N. Maple St., a building steeped in Murfreesboro history. Closed Sunday and Monday, Marina's is open 11am to 9 pm Tuesday-Thursday and until 9:30 pm Friday-Saturday. Call 615-849-8881.

Caroline's Victorian Café

When Karlene Sullivan moved from the East Coast to the small town of Crossville, she brought with her the recipes handed down from her mother, grandmother and aunts. She learned to cook as a young girl, watching her mother create delicious German and Polish dishes, many of which she serves in her café today. Caroline's Victorian Café, 750 70 E. Plaza #105, was named in honor of Karlene's mother, who was the inspiration for this new venture in her life. After retiring from a nursing career, Karlene opened the café with the help of her entire family, and they are all still an integral part of the business today. In fact, that (and the food, of course) is what makes this place so popular. From the beautiful handpainted roses on the front window to the special way each customer is treated, the entire experience is wonderful.

The atmosphere is warm and friendly—very casual during the day and a bit more dressy for dinner. The food is absolutely delicious, from the early morning breakfast, which includes Karlene's homemade Banana Nut Bread, to lunch and dinner, which feature wonderful salads, sandwiches, soups and hot dishes. Two of the most popular and requested items are the fabulous "Georgia Sunrise" soup and the homemade Bread Pudding.

Caroline's Victorian Café is the type of place where you'll see a wide variety of customers, from businessmen and women to lunching ladies on their day out. In fact, Caroline's is a popular choice for the "Red Hat Ladies!" The restaurant is open Monday-Saturday 6 am-9 pm. For additional information call 931-707-7765.

BIG BOY'S BARBEQUE

Don't be afraid to ask owners Kelly and Barbara Shepherd how they prepare Big Boy's famous barbeque. They'll even take you out to the pit and show you how it's done! That's one reason you'll feel more like you're eating in a friend's home than in a restaurant. Kelly says that his most memorable childhood times revolved around summer picnics and barbeques, and when the Shepherds got married, a charcoal grill was their first purchase. Big Boy's has perfected the art of "Hickory Smoked Pulled Pork," which literally falls off the bone. The neon "Eat Big Boy's BBQ" sign at 5409 Peavine Rd. in Crossville, invites customers to dine in or carryout. The friendly bantering among the Shepherd family inside is charming and entertaining. Open Monday-Saturday 10 am-7:30 pm. Call 931-484-1350.

Known for superb food at reasonable prices, Through the Grapevine is a restaurant, banquet suite, and catering service that will delight your senses. Offering gourmet items like delicious truffles, specialty cakes, and homemade Casseroles To Go for people in a hurry, owner Barbara Lester has created a restaurant that has been voted Best Caterer and Favorite New Restaurant in Rutherford County. Through the Grapevine, 630 Broadmor Blvd. in Murfreesboro, is open 9 am-4 pm Monday-Friday, serving lunch 11 am-2 pm. For more information, visit www.throughthegrapevine.net online or call 615-890-7346.

Wines & Wineries

HIGHLAND MANOR

TENNESSEE'S OLDEST WINERY

Rising out of the thick woodland in the heart of Tennessee's wild Cumberland Plateau is Highland Manor, Tennessee's oldest winery, 2965 S. York Hwy. in Jamestown. A beautiful rose arch welcomes visitors into the unique English Tudor winery known for producing fine handcrafted wines that have been honored by critical acclaim and awards. Owners Gertie and Butch Campbell delight in introducing friends to the pleasure of fine wine through tours of the entire wine-making process— from the "grape crushing area" to the cool, lantern-lit wine cellar. Select your favorite wine; match it with cheese, summer sausage, and crackers; and choose a beautiful picnic site on the grounds. Open Monday-Saturday 9 am-5 pm and Sunday 11 am-5 pm. Visit online www.highlandmanorwinery.com or call 931-879-9519.

As you explore the beautiful Cumberland Plateau, be sure to plan a visit to the Stonehaus Winery, 2444 Genesis Rd., #103. Located at the top of the plateau in Crossville, this beautiful stone building includes the winery and gift shop, a cheese pantry, and a restaurant. The winery is open seven days a week year-round from 9 am-7 pm and Sunday noon-5 pm. Taste the fine wines and then watch a video tour of the winery. You'll see all aspects of the winemaking process from the crushing of the grapes (not the way Lucy did) to the bottling process. The gift shop features wine racks and accessories, homemade fudge, and gourmet foods. Have a delicious lunch at the Deli, or a more elegant dinner by romantic candlelight at the Halcyon Days Restaurant. Sheltered picnic facilities are also available for a more leisurely day. Contact General Manager Belle Ramsey at 931-484-9463(WINE) or visit www.stonehauswinery.com.

Famous Tennessean

Sgt. Alvin C. York (1887-1964) — known as the "Turkey Hunter" and a WWI hero. He single handedly killed 25 Germans, knocked out 35 machine guns, and captured over 132 German prisoners during the "Battle of the Argonne Forest" in France in 1918 by using the "hunting skills" he acquired as a boy growing up in rural Tennessee. He returned to a hero's welcome, at the Crossville Depot, as depicted in the movie "Sgt. York" starring Gary Cooper.

DISCOVER DICKSON

"Mile Post 42"—That was the original name given to Dickson, Tennessee during the 1860s, when it was nothing more than a building that was used as an office for the construction of the railroad from White Bluff to the Tennessee River. In 1867, Mr. Conrad Berringer purchased the land that is now Dickson and had the town plotted. Dickson was almost completely destroyed by fire twice in its early history, once in 1893 and again in 1905. The town struggled through the years, as most small towns did at that time, building schools, churches, and business offices, as well as installing streetlights and parking meters. A movie theater opened in 1929. Natural gas was turned on in 1949. And, Dickson got its first hospital, Goodlark Hospital, in 1957.

Dickson has indeed grown and prospered over the years, into a city with a heart for the arts. The Renaissance Center is a state-of-the-art facility, which promotes a variety of educational programs in a place where both children and adults can experience a "renaissance" of learning. It was built by Dr. L.C. William and Dr. Jimmy Jackson, the same brothers who also built the Goodlark Hospital. In building the Renaissance Center, the "Jackson Foundation" was responsible for the birth of one of Tennessee's most innovative fine arts and technology learning centers, bringing music, art, theater, 3-D animation, and computer technology to the city of Dickson.

For more information about Dickson, contact the Dickson County Chamber of Commerce at 615-446-2349, or visit www.dicksoncountychamber.com online.

Dickson Fairs Festivals & Fun

February
Valentine Tea & Dinner
Princess Tea

March
St. Patty's Tea

May
First Weekend in May

June
Dickson County Invitational
Fiddlers Contest
Relay for Life
Stampede Rodeo Days

July
White Bluff Festival
July 4th Celebration

August
Charlotte Festival

September
Antique Auto Show

October
Cumberland Furnace Fall Festival

November
Christmas in Dickson County

December
Christmas Parade
White Bluff Christmas

Antiques

Main Street Antique Mall and Deli

A visit to Main Street Antique Mall and Deli, 131 N. Main St. in Dickson, is a little like stepping back into time. Outside the front door on the sidewalk, antique items give the market a "1940s General Store" feeling. Just inside the door, you'll find the Deli, with vintage décor that inspires nostalgia.

In opening Main Street Antiques, owner Billie Weisenfels was determined to create the kind of place she loved to shop. She wanted it to be a place visitors could browse at leisure, find unique items for their homes and gardens, or just be inspired with new decorating ideas. With more than 12,000-square-feet of floor space, you'll be hard pressed to see everything in one visit—and that means you'll be back again and again. She carries American and European antiques, collectibles, and primitives, Shabby Chic, as well as flea market finds. The booths are constantly changing and evolving, so each visit is a new experience. The wide array of eclectic furniture and furnishings will help you add "layers" of personality, style, and, of course, history to your home. Iron trellises, benches and beautiful garden furniture help provide the perfect atmosphere for "outside living" in Dickson's pleasant climate. Billie has also acquired an elite line of functional hand-crafted art pottery by a well-known Mississippi artist, and the exclusive Wax Stax Galore Candles.

Best of all, when you're through shopping, you can treat yourself to a delicious lunch, an old-fashioned milkshake, or coffee and dessert. One of the most popular items on the menu is the delicious "Corn Bread Salad," but everything is wonderful.

Main Street Antiques is open Monday-Saturday 9 am-5 pm. Call 615-441-3633 for more information.

STUDIO 123

When Beverly Caldwell decided to open Studio 123 in 1995 to showcase her work and that of her friends—it was a leap of faith! Over the years, the shop has grown to include the artwork of many local artists, as well as artists from all over the country. You'll find handcrafted jewelry from more than 20 designers, as well as pottery, garden art and candles. Visit Beverly and her mother at 123 N. Main St. in Dickson, Monday-Friday 10 am-5:30 pm and Saturday until 5 pm. Call 615-446-7215.

Jo Ann's

Everything about Jo Ann's Gifts and Home Accents, 114 N. Main St. in Dickson, is inviting. From the beautiful displays of Arthur Court and Wilton Armetale to the exquisite bottles and decanters of Lady Primrose products for the luxurious bath—you'll love this store! Jo Ann's carries crystal and china, as well as linens, home accents, and fashion jewelry. Stop by Monday-Saturday 10 am-5 pm. For more information, contact Jo Ann at 615-446-2946.

Miss Martha's Mercantile

Miss Martha's Mercantile is much more than a place to buy gifts and fine linens. This store is a place to truly experience yesteryear. You'll be able to touch the linens and learn how to care for them, as well. You'll also find music boxes, handmade quilts, tapestry wall hangings and more! Miss Martha's Mercantile, 120 N. Main in Dickson, is open Monday-Friday 9 am-5 pm and Saturday until 4 pm. For more information, call 615-740-8500.

THE FRONT PORCH
on Center Avenue, LLC

The 103-year-old Victorian home at 108 Center Ave. has been transformed into a cozy, charming, and cheerful café that has fast become a Dickson favorite. The old fireplaces and antique furnishings make diners feel as though they are lunching in a friend's home. Carol Michael had been catering from her home for more than 15 years when she decided to open this wonderful restaurant. She has managed to combine the elements of fine "country cooking" with a twist of gourmet, and she takes great care to present quality foods that uphold Southern traditions. A Blue Plate special is prepared each day, with homemade soups, salads, sandwiches, and delectable desserts rounding out the menu. The "Back Porch" is open after hours offering frozen casseroles, salads, and soups for pickup. The restaurant is open Sunday-Friday 11 am-2 pm and Friday evenings 5-8:30 pm. Call 615-441-0006.

With a love of great coffee and creative cuisine, and a fun spirit, Jeremy and Holly Spencer opened House~Blend at 124 N. Main St. in Dickson. House~Blend offers gourmet coffee drinks and smoothies, a unique menu of fresh sandwiches, salads and soups, and a fun and eclectic assortment of gifts. Open Monday-Thursday 6 am-6 pm, Friday until 10 pm, and Saturday 9 am-6 pm. Visit www.houseblendonline.com or call 615-446-3311. Also, visit in Columbia at 420 W. 7th St. or, call 931-540-0555.

Blest Friends Boutique

Blending their love of fashion and art along with their expertise in marketing and merchandising, friends Paige Perry and Lisa Stansfield opened the trendy, very successful Blest Friends Boutique at 134 N. Main St. in Dickson. They've been best friends since 1989, with one very fun thing in common—they both love to shop! From the vast array of jewelry and accessories to the clothing lines featuring everything from casual to business and elegant to funky, you will love shopping every corner of this large store. Whether you're a Miss, Petite, or Plus size, you're sure to find something you will love. Open Tuesday-Saturday 10 am-5 pm. If all the shopping works up an appetite, Paige also owns the Cajun Café, serving authentic Cajun cuisine with mouthwatering dishes such as jambalaya, gumbo and crawfish, located conveniently behind the boutique. Call 615-441-6151 or visit www.blestfriendsboutique.com online.

Hotels

Just a short drive from Nashville and a short walk from the great restaurants in Dickson, you'll find the Comfort Inn by Choice Hotels, 1025 E. Christi Dr. From the usually occupied rocking chairs on the "front porch" to the heated indoor pool, families love the personal touches and wonderful customer service that makes the Comfort Inn a lodging favorite. The king, queen or double rooms open to interior corridors, and feature free local calls, a data port, a coffee maker, an iron and ironing board, a hair dryer, a refrigerator, a microwave, and a 27-inch color television. A delicious continental breakfast is served each morning in the lobby, and guests receive a free daily newspaper. Call 615-441-5252, toll free 800-4CHOICE, or visit www.choicehotels.com online.

DISCOVER FAYETTEVILLE/LYNCHBURG/ SHELBYVILLE

FAYETTEVILLE

Fayetteville has a community motto, "Where Tradition Meets Tomorrow!" It is the county seat for Lincoln County, and it's located in southern Middle Tennessee about 78 miles south of Nashville. The original 100-acre tract of land that gave birth to Fayetteville was purchased in 1810 for only $100. Quite a deal, eh? The name for this new community was chosen in honor of the many settlers who came to the beautiful area from Fayetteville, N.C. History dates back to an even earlier time though, with evidence of hunters as early as 1784, and even further back to 1540 when Spanish explorer DeSoto camped at this village.

Then and Now

In March of 1814, during the War of 1812, the Tennessee Militia encamped in Fayetteville near four ancient oak trees—which are still standing today. The troops were traveling to Alabama in order to fight in the now infamous Battle of Horseshoe Bend. The Tennessee Militia was comprised of such noted figures as, Major General Andrew Jackson, Sam Houston and David Crocket.

Fortunately, the town of Fayetteville managed to escape total devastation during the Civil War and has continued to thrive through the years and become a city of both historic and modern prosperity. The Town Square has a wonderful history as a marketplace. It is alive with exciting shopping, historic commercial architecture, city festivals, and lots of sweet Southern charm. You will be warmly welcomed at many scenic and historic attractions such as the Lincoln County Museum, which is located in the Old Borden Milk Plant on Main Avenue South. This museum is a "bridge to connect the past, present and future," with military, medical, and agricultural exhibits from days gone by.

Antiques Galore!

And, if you love antiques, you'll love shopping the historic Town Square. There are more antique shops per square mile than anywhere else in the area. You'll find clothiers, jewelers, gift shops, fabric stores and, of course, antique shops! You'll also discover a delightful, old-fashioned movie theater. You won't be surprised to learn that many of Fayetteville's downtown shops have been featured in *Southern Living Magazine*. For example, don't miss Sir's Fabrics at 110 Elk Ave. N., just off the square. Sir's Fabrics began in 1948 and is now on both sides of the street. The selection of upholstery, drapery and apparel fabrics will amaze you, and Sir's prices are great! Be sure to bring your swatches.

There are wonderful events planned in Fayetteville throughout the year. Don't miss the Freedom Days Festival in July, the Lincoln County Fair in September, or the Host of Christmas Past in November.

LYNCHBURG

This tiny Tennessee town is definitely not a place you will stumble upon accidentally. It is truly "off the beaten path," but well worth your time. It is a charming, slow-moving town filled with history and charm. Life seems to move more slowly in Lynchburg. It is a town lined with "hills and history," and one that has changed very little over the years. The magnificent rolling Tennessee hills and beautiful horse and cattle farms are a delight to the senses— such beauty! The locals are quite friendly, too. As you travel the roads around Lynchburg, don't be surprised if someone you don't know actually *waves* to you! Go ahead—wave back, or better yet, wave and nod. It feels great! You won't find strip malls, fast food drive-ins or famous super stores. What you *will* find are delightful antique shops and gift boutiques—all family-owned and Tennessee friendly.

The town's most famous attraction is, of course, the main reason thousands of visitors find their way to Lynchburg each year. Lynchburg is home to the Jack Daniel's Distillery. Every drop of Jack Daniel's Whiskey has been made here since Mr. Jack Daniel himself perfected the process in 1866. Plan a fascinating tour of the distillery, and perhaps sample a little of the famous "Lynchburg Lemonade!"

SHELBYVILLE

Say the word "Shelbyville," and people immediately think of horses. Not just ordinary horses, but a distinctive, high-stepping show horse—"The Tennessee Walking Horse." The Tennessee Walking Horse breed developed in this area during the late 19th century, and became known for its rhythmic and gliding gait. These horses were originally intended for farm work, but grew into a handsome, pleasure mount and show horse. Today, they are the pride of Tennessee. Shelbyville has been hosting the world's largest Walking Horse show for more than 60 years, and has acquired the title of "The Walking Horse Capital of the World." The Tennessee Walking Horse National Celebration is held in the fall each year in beautiful Shelbyville, drawing thousands of visitors from around the nation to watch the world-renowned breed "strut its stuff." The celebrated event usually lasts 11 days with the award-winning new World Grand Champion being named on the last day. It is a cherished tradition and a civic marvel that has united the community and brought fame to this verdant part of Middle Tennessee.

To The Point

Although the Walking Horse Celebration takes center ring in Shelbyville during the fall, the town "made its mark" back in 1916 as headquarters for the Musgrave Pencil Company. The founder, James Raford Musgrave, began trading farmers new post-and-wire fencing for their old cedar fence posts, then milled them and turned them into quality pencil stock. Today, the company produces more than 500,000 pencils each day and ships them throughout the

United States and Europe. You'll find lots and lots of yellow pencils to be sure, but also you'll discover the Musgrave Pencil Company manufactures everything from glow-in-the dark to holiday to company logo pencils. They like to say, "Musgrave's got the *write* stuff!" Shelbyville was named "Pencil City, USA" by Governor Buford Ellington in the 1950s.

Setting The Standard

Shelbyville also boasts an exquisite town square. Shelbyville's courthouse square is called a "block central courthouse square," and has been coined as "The Shelbyville Plan." It was plotted in 1810— a grid pattern with the courthouse as the centerpiece and four equal sides of commercial buildings. The plan was so simple and easy to use that new towns began to model their own downtown areas after Shelbyville, and it became known as a prototype for town squares across the country. Remember the town of Shelbyville the next time you drive "around a town square." The Shelbyville Square is listed on the National Register of Historic Places, and most of the early buildings are still standing. Early settlers selected a high point of land on which to settle, and the courthouse was built at the center of that high ground. The beautiful Bedford County Courthouse is the first thing you'll see as you enter the town—both the figurative and literal heart of the city. In recent years, there has been a surge of revitalization in the Shelbyville downtown area, which charms visitors and residents alike. From hometown furniture shops to quaint antique malls and delightful eateries, the old-fashioned shops of Shelbyville offer exciting shopping and unique treasures.

For additional information about Fayetteville, contact the Fayetteville and Lincoln County Chamber of Commerce at 931-433-1234 or visit www.vallnet.com/chamberofcommerce online.

For additional information about Lynchburg, contact the Lynchburg Moore County Chamber of Commerce at 931-759-4111 or visit www.lynchburgtenn.com online.

For additional information about Shelbyville, contact the Shelbyville Bedford County, Tennessee Chamber at 888-662-2525, 931-684-3482 or visit www.shelbyvilletn.com online.

Fayetteville Fairs Festivals & Fun

April
  Easter Egg Eggstravaganza

May
  Kiwanis Pancake Breakfast

June
  Dairy Day on the Square

July
  Freedom Days Festival

September
  Lincoln County Fair
  Lincoln County Bluegrass &
    Crafts Festival

November
  Host of Christmas Past

Lynchburg Fairs Festivals & Fun

May
  Spring in the Hollow
  Spotted Saddle Horse Show

June
  Motor Cycle Rally
  Frontier Days

July
  Tennessee Walking Horse
    Show

August
  Spotted Saddle Horse Show

September
  Whiskey Runners Car Show

October
  Jack Daniel's Barbeque Contest

December
  Christmas in Lynchburg

Shelbyville Fairs Festivals & Fun

March
SSHBEA Sport Horse Winter
Games

May
SSHBEA Spring Show

June
Racking Horse Classic

July
International Ponies of the
Americas National Show

August
Tennessee Walking Horse
National Celebration
Bedford County Fair

September
SSHBEA World Grand
Championship

October
Fall Food Festival

November
Holiday Mixer
SSHBEA Sport Horse World
Grand Championship

December
Christmas Parade

P the OMEGRANATE

Gifts • Antiques • Decorative Accessories

You will love browsing this wonderful gift and antique shop at 107 Public Sq. S. in Shelbyville. Bob and Jo Newton take pride in having been in business for more than 16 years in this historic town square location. The Pomegranate features high quality lamps and home accessories to fun collectibles like Christopher Radko and Byer's Choice Carolers. The selection is remarkable. Open Monday-Saturday 9 am-5 pm. For more information, call 931-684-3673.

DISTILLERY-VISITOR CENTER

Established in 1866, world-famous Jack Daniel's is America's oldest registered distillery. Tucked away from the main road in the Tennessee hills, it's just a short walk from the Lynchburg Hardware & General Store and the Barrel Shop on the square in Lynchburg.

This Tennessee hollow features a visitor center crafted from limestone and wood where you can sit and relax near the spring-fed waters of Mulberry Creek or take an unforgettable free tour of the distillery.

This historic distillery, listed on the National Register of Historic Places, is home of the best-selling American-made whiskey in the world—Jack Daniel's Old No.7 Brand Tennessee Whiskey. Located off Hwy. 55 at 182 Lynchburg Hwy., the visitor center and distillery are open 9 am-4:30 pm, 360 days-a-year. Call 931-759-6356 or visit www.jackdaniels.com online.
(Color photo featured in front section of book.)

Belle du Jour
Bed & Breakfast

Every day is beautiful at Belle du Jour, where you will enjoy Southern hospitality with a touch of love, peace and joy. This is Owner Kimberly Churn's vision and she is dedicated to providing it for her guests. With comfortable rooms, private baths and excellent local cuisine, you'll fall in love with this historic bed and breakfast situated at the edge of Shelbyville's historic district.

Belle du Jour Bed & Breakfast, 300 E. Lane St., is open seven days a week. The tea room is open for lunch Sunday-Friday 11 am-2 pm and dinner Friday-Saturday 4-11 pm. Call 931-684-3894.

The Tigress

The shop is small, but remember, wonderful things come in small packages! The Tigress is proof of that! Located at 132 E. College St. in Fayetteville, The Tigress is one of those remarkable little boutiques that's sure to become one of your favorite places to shop for unique clothing and wonderful accessories. Owner Dianne Sumners says that great customer service has been paramount to the success of the boutique. They still special order, ship, do alterations, offer complimentary gift-wrap, and take telephone orders. Repeat customers are even invited to take items home on approval! You will love the distinctive clothing lines and fun accessories. And, you'll also adore the wonderful selection of gifts and beautiful Italian pottery by Vietri. The Tigress is open Monday 10 am-5:30 pm, Tuesday-Friday until 6 pm and Saturday until 5 pm. Call 931-433-8735.

Four stores under one roof at 766 N. Main St.—yes! Visit Carolyn's/Simmons (931-684-4411) for the most wonderful ladies' clothing and accessories. Lowery Jewelers (931-684-8623) showcases fine jewelry, and decorative accessories; and The Knit Kit (931-684-4596) offers needlework classes, books, and many yarns. Enjoy Charleston décor and the most delicious lunch in Shelbyville at Charleston on Main tearoom (931-680-1832). Open Monday-Saturday 9 am-5 pm.

Furniture

Jack Daniel's uses only American White Oak to make their whiskey barrels because of their porosity and unique chemical composition. But they only use them one time. So what do you do with a whiskey barrel after you've drained the last drop? Visit the Jack Daniel's Barrel Shop in Lynchburg's historical square, just minutes away from the distillery and visitors center. The clever folks here have taken the whiskey barrels and crafted them into unique products like home bars, CD cases, rocking chairs, planters, and even poker tables. These are beautiful pieces that will last a lifetime, and of course will make wonderful conversation pieces. You can take part of Tennessee's Jack Daniel's legend home with you. We did! The Barrel Shop is open Monday-Saturday 9 am-5 pm and Sunday 1-5 pm. For information, call 931-759-6370 or visit www.jackdaniels.com. *(Color photo featured in front section of book.)*

Jean's Lawn and Landscape, Inc.

 Brad Jean bought his grandfather's pickup truck when he was in high school, loaded his lawn mower and tools in the back, and voila! His landscape business was born! He said he has always loved "getting his hands in the dirt." That's exactly what he has been doing for more than 10 years at Jean's Lawn & Landscape, 2668 Huntsville Hwy. in Fayetteville. With a degree in Plant and Soil Services and Business Administration from Middle Tennessee State University, Brad has grown his business into a thriving landscape design and maintenance company, offering complete service to commercial and residential properties. From a high school kid with a pickup truck to a company of 22 employees, Jean's Lawn & Landscape is a success. Brad attributes it to hard work, loyal customers, and the support of his beautiful wife Shena. The office is open Monday-Saturday 8 am-5 pm. Call Brad at 931-433-8897.

R.D. WILLIAMS GIFTS & FRAMING

Three generations of a wonderful Tennessee family have worked side-by-side through the years to make R.D. Williams Gifts & Framing one of the most successful and loved businesses in Fayetteville. R. D. and Kathaleen Williams opened the doors to the gift and framing shop in 1948 on the south side of the square. After R.D.'s death in 1963, and son R.D. Jr.'s death in Vietnam in 1966, Kathaleen and daughters Linda and Brenda moved the store to the Winchester Hwy. When Kathaleen passed away in 1996, Brenda and husband Ernie Roles built the log building it occupies today at 1560 Winchester Hwy. You'll find replacement lamp shades, Fenton Art Glass, an amazing collection of unique collectibles, and original pottery by artist Jennie Roles Walter. The shop is open Monday-Saturday 9 am-5 pm and in December, Sunday 1-5 pm. Call 931-433-3211 for more information.

SULLY'S GIFTS & TENNESSEE STUFF

As you enter Sully's Gifts, located on Public Sq. W. in Lynchburg, you'll be greeted by a display of carved wooden Indian figures, Jack Daniel's memorabilia, and antique jugs and bottles. Owner/manager James Sullenger opened Sully's Gifts when he retired from the aerospace industry in 1988. Later, he opened Tennessee Stuff just down the street on Public Sq. W. too! Both shops are open 9 am-5 pm daily. For more information, call 931-759-4661 or 931-759-4647.

Prissy's

Named for her adorable Yorkie, Prissy, Kathy Potter's rather eclectic gift boutique at 601 N. Main St. in Shelbyville is a great place to shop for unique gifts and treats. Prissy's carries Blue Sky Collectibles, Yankee Candles, beautiful pottery, jewelry, and great bath and body products. Fabulous gift baskets are Kathy's specialty—either ready or custom made. The store is open Monday-Friday 10 am-6 pm and Saturday until 4 pm. Call 931-684-8882.

Colleen's Cottage

gifts and accessories

Colleen Embry keeps a special index file for her customers' wish lists, so you are sure to find the perfect gift every time! Each room of this charming clapboard cottage gift shop at 103 Collier Ave. in Shelbyville is filled with collectible kitchen items and cookbooks, jewelry and fashion accessories, garden delights, and beautiful tabletop decorations. Stop by Colleen's Cottage Monday-Saturday 9 am-5:30 pm. For more information, call 931-685-0012.

Family-owned Dancy's, 112 Public Sq. E. in Shelbyville, is an inviting shop for the young and the young at heart! You'll find birthday presents, bridal gifts, and charming home accessories. With a beautiful selection of Crabtree & Evelyn bath and body products and a full line of Capezio body and footwear, it's a fun place to shop. Dance lessons are taught at Dancy's too! Open 10 am-5 pm Monday-Friday and 9 am-2 pm on Saturday, with extended holiday hours. Call 931-684-6223.

You'll find a vast range of Jack Daniel's souvenirs including clothing, glassware, and curios, at the Lynchburg

Hardware & General Store in the main historic square, near the distillery and visitor center. Open 9 am-5 pm Monday-Saturday and 1-5 pm Sunday. Call 931-759-4200 for more information.

 ## LYNCHBURG DRUG STORE

Established in 1910, Lynchburg Drug Store is a slice of true Americana. The old-fashioned soda fountain, with its brass stools and gleaming fixtures, will take you back in time as you enjoy one of owner Bob Gray's thick, luscious milkshakes. Don't miss this treasure!

Lynchburg Drug Store, Public Square E. in historic Lynchburg, is open Monday-Friday 9 am-5 pm. Call 931-759-7329.

CARTER'S DRUG STORE

Customers tell us, "If Carter's doesn't have it, nobody will!" Carter's Drug Store, 106 S. Elk Ave. in Fayetteville, has been in business since the late 1800s. And, owner Wayne Damron has been a pharmacist at Carter's for more than 34 years. Today, several family members work with him. This all-inclusive pharmacy/gift shop is a one-stop market. Visit Carter's Monday-Friday 8 am-7 pm, Saturday until 6 pm, and Sunday 10-5 pm. For more information, call 931-433-1511.

Inns & Hotels

LYNCHBURG COUNTRY INN

This is country-cottage comfort with all of the amenities of a modern motel. The Lynchburg Country Inn, 423 Majors Blvd. on Hwy. 55 (just a half mile south of the town's only traffic light), is surrounded by the beautiful countryside of Moore County. There are 24 spotless rooms, including handicap accessible accommodations; all moderately priced. We liked having a refrigerator, hair dryer, and coffee maker in the room, as well as data ports for computer needs. The Inn is conveniently located close to the town square shopping area and the Jack Daniel's Distillery. For more information, call 931-759-5995, 866-759-5995 or visit www.lynchburgcountryinn.com.

 Conveniently situated one mile north of Shelbyville's city center at 1607 N. Main St. (also known as Hwy. 231), the Country Hearth Inn offers tastefully decorated cottage-style rooms with a complimentary continental breakfast. Or, for a romantic get-away, reserve a hot-tub suite. The Country Hearth Inn was just recently built, so the accommodations are in excellent condition and awaiting your arrival. For reservations, call 931-680-1030.

BEST WESTERN FAYETTEVILLE INN & TROTTER'S RESTAURANT

It is located high on a hill, only one mile from the charming downtown Fayetteville shopping district, and features one of the most popular restaurants in the area. The family-owned-and-operated Best Western Fayetteville Inn, 3021 Thornton-Taylor Pkwy., offers 64 beautifully appointed rooms with all of the amenities of home. Facilities and services include: a swimming pool, meeting rooms, data ports, iron and ironing boards, coffee makers, and room service. Trotter's Restaurant serves hundreds of hometown people daily—it's a favorite! For more information or reservations, call 931-433-0100, 800-780-7234, or visit www.bestwestern.com.

Jewelry

Heritage Jewelers

Heritage Jewelers at 108 Public Sq. E. has been an institution in Shelbyville since the early 1980s, but the Hix family has been involved in the Shelbyville historic square since the 1900s. In fact, their beautiful jewelry store is located on the square with the historic "J.H. Hix" block. We loved the custom-made equestrian jewelry. Stop by Monday-Friday 9 am-5:15 pm and Saturday until 3 pm. Visit www.herjeweler.com or call 931-684-3115 or 888-240-0585.

O'Houlihans

Step back in time for a scrumptious meal at O'Houlihans on Fayetteville's public square at 101 E. Market St. Enjoy hot or cold deli sandwiches on fresh baked rolls, mouth-watering soups, and crisp salads in a century-old building, complete with an antique safe, an old-time cash register, and hardwood floors. We loved the German Chocolate Upside Down Cake. YUM! Open Monday-Saturday 8 am-5:30 pm. For more information, call 931-433-0557.

Cheddar—hand-dipped the old fashioned way in red or black wax—as well as Edam, Gouda, and Jalapeno Pepper Jack! With more than 65 years in business, Bedford Cheese, 111 Deery St. in Shelbyville, is a cheese lover's paradise! Owners Joe and Martha Madeo offer top-quality cheese products, cakes, meats, and gift baskets. Open 8 am-5 pm Monday-Friday and 9 am-1 pm on Saturday. For more information, call 931-684-5422, 800-264-0115 or visit www.bedfordcheese.com online.

LEGENDS RESTAURANT

Be sure to check out Legends Restaurant in Shelbyville at 1609 N. Main St. See page 231 for full details.

DISCOVER FRANKLIN

It is said to be ". . . 100 years and a few short miles from Nashville." Franklin, Tennessee, is a town steeped in the history of the Civil War, with beautiful Victorian and antebellum architecture; a canvas for some of God's most breathtaking natural handiwork; and a place where hospitality is a natural state of being. Visitors to this charming town immediately feel like long-time friends and honored guests as they explore historic downtown shopping areas, tour the sites of Civil War history, or enjoy the abundance of recreational facilities available.

Savor The History and The Shopping

The county seat of Williamson County, Franklin is a picturesque little town set among gentle rolling hills, magnificent horse farms, and the Harpeth River. Franklin has been voted the "Best Small Town in Tennessee," and is a Tennessee Main Street Community under the National Trust for Historic Preservation. The Victorian commercial district is the heart of Franklin and offers a wonderful mix of antique shops, art galleries, clothiers, and gift stores. The commemorative brick sidewalks and renovated historic buildings house the most wonderful boutiques and eateries. You can tour many of the buildings and homes, which were built during the days of prosperity before the Civil War. Guided or private tours are perfect for the entire family to enjoy.

There are three particular Franklin tours that enlighten visitors to the city's fascinating past. A daytime walking tour will show you a church for freed slaves, the antebellum courthouse, The Confederate statue, and St. Paul's Episcopal Church. A night tour called the "Ghosts and Gore Tour" looks at a few rather "sordid" happenings in Franklin's past, including bootlegging, lynchings, public whippings and hangings, street corner shootings, and assorted "activities of the night."

Memorials and Museums

There is a story everywhere you look; especially in the homes that experienced firsthand the drama and brutality of the Civil War. On November 30, 1864, the bloody and tragic Battle of Franklin began when Confederate soldiers charged entrenched Union soldiers near the "Carter House" and died by the thousands. The battle raged for more than five hours in the middle of Franklin, where more than 6,000 Confederate and 2,000 Union soldiers perished. This home served as the Federal Command Post, while the family hid in the basement. A visit to this historic battlefield includes a video presentation and a guided tour of the house and grounds. The Carnton Plantation is another beautiful, historic home that witnessed the carnage of the war. The home was used to provide shelter for injured and dying Confederate soldiers. One soldier wrote, "...And when the noble old house could hold no more, the yard was appropriated until the wounded and dead filled that..." After the war, John and Carrie McGavock designated almost two acres of their land as a Confederate Cemetery for those fallen soldiers. Be sure to visit each of these lovely homes during your visit to Franklin, and catch a glimpse of a picture of how each played a pivotal part in American history.

Don't miss a visit to the new African-American Museum in Franklin, which shows the struggles, triumphs, and incredible contributions of African-Americans in Williamson County.

Shop 'Til You Drop

And, saving the best information for last—great shopping! Franklin is an antique phenomenon, making the national top 10 list of "greatest undiscovered areas for antiquing." The Factory at Franklin is a complex of 11 Depression-era buildings that have been renovated into a Tennessee shopping mecca! Restaurants, antique shops, art galleries, theaters, clubs, and more beckon visitors who *love* to shop. You will also love the downtown shopping area, with quaint boutiques, fine dining and an enchanted atmosphere. Can you say, "Shop 'til you drop?"

Franklin is just such a wonderful place to visit. It is an exciting, friendly town, steeped in history that comes alive in a beautiful way, filled with treasures to be discovered, and memories to be made.

For more information about Franklin, contact the Williamson County Convention and Visitors Bureau at 800-356-3445 or 615-794-1225 or visit www.williamsoncvb.org online.

Franklin
Fairs Festivals & Fun

March
> St. Patrick's Brew, Stew and Stroll

April
> Main Street Festival

May
> Tennessee Renaissance Festival
> Franklin Rotary Club Rodeo
> Town and Country Tour of Homes
> LPGA Tournament

June
> Historic Carnton's Sunset Concert Series (June-
> September)

July
> Franklin on the Fourth
> Fiddling on the Harpeth
> Bluegrass Festival

September
> Southern Folklife Festival

October
> The Music City Futurity Cutting Horse Show
> Pumpkin Fest

November
> Veterans Day Parade

December
> Christmas Parade
> Carter House Candlelight Tour of Homes
> Dickens of a Christmas

Unique Shops at

The **FACTORY** *at Franklin*

For the gift with attitude, **Cherie's Unique Collection** proudly stocks elegant, distinctive, and whimsical items from around the world. Call 615-599-9904.

Annette Charles, a "true boutique" offers designer lines not found in department or chain stores. And, fashion jewelry that is unsurpassed in Franklin. Call 615-595-2020.

The Stoveworks Restaurant serves homemade casseroles, soups, salads, sandwiches and desserts. Call 615-791-6065.

Viking Culinary Arts Center brings gourmet essentials,

cookware, cutlery tools, and hands-on cooking schools. Call 615-599-9617.

Whether it's a medical facial, a relaxing massage, or a package combining both, avail yourself of **Just Be Spa**'s physician-directed programs. Call 615-261-0350.

Artifex is a multi-media fine craft gallery with works of local, national and international artisans. Call 615-599-1022.

The **Stonebridge Gallery** offers original oil paintings, limited edition prints and nationally and internationally known artists. Call toll-free 877-790-9020 or 615-790-9020.

Color specialist and stylist Rodney Mitchell of **Rodney Mitchell Salon**, brings the best products and innovations to his clients, which include Faith Hill and Tim McGraw. Call 615-599-0559.

Plum Delicious is stocked with irresistible, moderately priced treasures. They specialize in creative custom gift baskets. Call 615-595-7586.

Visit **Stone Angel** for a collection of home, garden and spiritual accents. Call 615-791-6343.

These unique businesses and many more are all located at **The Factory at Franklin**, 230 Franklin Rd. Most are open 10 am-5 pm Monday-Thursday; 10 am-6 pm Friday-Saturday; and 1-5 pm Sunday. Visit www.factoryatfranklin.com or call 615-791-1777.

Shop ... Dine ... Unwind
at the Factory at Franklin

WALTON'S

ANTIQUE & ESTATE JEWELRY

One of Franklin's sparkling jewels stands alone as a premiere antique and estate jewelry boutique—Walton's Antique & Estate Jewelry, 410 Main St. This Franklin tradition had its beginnings in 1974 when Melba Walton opened the store in the downtown historic building. Her son Mike Walton joined her as a Bench Jeweler in 1982, and in 1984 earned his Graduate Gemologist Certificate. Today Melba and Mike work side-by-side along with Mike's wife Peggy (also a Graduate Gemologist) and two jewelers. Mike continues to travel the country to estate sales and auctions, bringing home one of a kind treasures and antique estate jewelry. You might find an original gypsy bracelet, a diamond dragonfly, or a solid gold purse! The walls are lined with gleaming antique sterling silver cups, trays, and wonderful gifts. The store is open Tuesday–Saturday 10 am-4:30 pm. For more information, call 615-790-0244.

Rozanne Jackson, Bo Boaz and Mary Clark have created an exciting, one-of-a-kind shopping experience in their beautiful, eclectic store—The Iron Gate. The building at 340 Main St. in Franklin is in itself a historical treasure. Built in 1900, it has a full basement that was actually once used by Al Capone as a "speakeasy!" The building's original brick walls, soaring ceilings, beautiful wood floors, and open skylights produce a timeless, elegant backdrop for all of the wonderful items you'll find inside.

Rozanne, Bo and Mary have an exciting mix of antiques, sofas and chairs, luxurious bedding, architectural elements, and unique chandeliers for every room in the house. Customers love that they can get custom designed as well as manufactured pieces, including: beds, ottomans, tables, and armoires made of wood, iron, or glass, or a combination of the three.

"Our interior decorator has a long list of very happy clients," says Bo Boaz. "Our buyer has traveled and lived around the world." You will love their genuine desire to help you find the perfect piece for your home. Everything in the store is unique and special, and the staff's decorating style is remarkable.

The Iron Gate also carries the entire line—all 42 scents—of Trapp Candles! Every poured candle is saturated with as much fragrance as possible—in essence, "a bottle of perfume in every candle." These candles fill the air with the most wonderful fragrances.

The Iron Gate is open Monday–Saturday 10 am to 5 pm and Sunday 1 to 5 pm seasonally. For more information, call 615-791-7511.

Katydid's

Kaye Lockwood says, "Katydid's rose like a phoenix from the ashes of my former life." Her father, Dexter Lockwood, had built a tremendously successful bridge construction company in the building at 1222 W. Main St. in Franklin, and Kaye or "Katydid" as her dad called her, tagged along behind him from the age of 10. She worked for him during all of her school holidays and vacations, and eventually fulltime after finishing college at Vanderbilt. When Mr. Lockwood died in 1995, Kaye ran the business for seven more years, but began to long for more. So she covered ceiling tiles in fabric; buttoned and tufted walls in velvet; learned to use a wet saw to install marble floors; sculpted the 30-year-old shrubs in front; and VOILA . . . an interior design shop was born.

Katydid's is a wonderfully unique place to shop, visit and sip gourmet coffee... offering services for every decorating need— designers, expert carpentry, workrooms, upholstery, faux painters, muralists, and carpet installation. Kaye carries high-end fabrics and trims not commonly found in the area, and she has an enormous inventory of silk, chenilles, trims and tassels. You'll find beautiful lamps and chandeliers (even alabaster,) imported lace sheers, hand-carved mahogany furniture as well as designer print carpets. There are walls of drapery hardware to suit any decor; oil paintings for every taste; whimsical jewelry; and handbags galore. For gentlemen shoppers, she stocks hand-rolled cigars from the Dominican Republic and French processed high gloss alligator accessories. Katydid's has a library of design books and a cozy kitchen table around which to gather. She boasts a line of cookbooks, gourmet pecans, cappuccino, cocoas, teas, soup mixes, and Victorian bath products. You will love meeting the amazing "Katydid" and shopping in this beautiful store. The store is open Tuesday–Friday 9 am-5 pm, and Saturday 10 am-4:30 pm. Call 615-794-8465.

MAYFIELD MW WALKER

Galleries LLC

Peggy Mayfield and Debbie Walker met each other 15 years ago through "antique world connections," and forged not only a lasting friendship, but also one of Franklin's most successful antique businesses. Their impressive collections of fine French, English, American, and Italian antiques are showcased in one of the town's most historic buildings at 347 Main St. You'll find exquisite antiques to furnish the most intimate settings to the largest banquet rooms—tables, sideboards, chests, dressers, antique porcelain and crystal, and a large selection of Old World antique lighting. The store is open Monday–Saturday 10 am-5 pm and by appointment. Call 615-794-4404. *(Color photo featured in front section of this book.)*

Along the Way

You will love meeting Margaret Miller and Susan Bonds, and browsing through every corner of Along the Way at 2181 Hillsboro Rd. in Franklin. Margaret says, "We have new art and furniture, old art and furniture, and local art and furniture."

From the whimsical collection of outdoor garden benches, wooden tables, and iron flower stands to the jewelry, rugs, and sweet baby gifts, you will love this store! Open Monday–Saturday 10 am-5 pm and Sunday 1-5 pm. Call 615-599-7742.

Artists & Art Galleries

artifex

Whether you buy a gift for yourself or a gift for someone else, make it a "Gift of Art." You can always find that special gift at Artifex, located in The Factory at Franklin, 230 Franklin Rd. 11-D. This gallery is a remarkable collection of multi-media artwork from local, national and international artists. Owner Brian Downey aspires to find art that refreshes and rejuvenates, while adding beauty to the homes and lives of all who shop in his store. Brian can assist you in accessorizing your home with original fine crafts by contemporary artists. Artifex—formerly Treasure Trove, owned by sisters Veta and Melissa Riddle—is carrying on the vision and the high quality of work customers have come to expect.

At Artifex you will find works in clay, as well as metal art, ranging from intricate sculptures to simple magnets. Glass lovers will be amazed at the large selection of hand-blown glass. Artifex also carries a selection of hand-crafted jewelry, with extraordinary pieces for every occasion—funky to formal—you will find it all! The gallery's hours are Monday-Thursday 10 am-5 pm and Friday-Saturday until 6 pm. For more information, call 615-599-1022.

Main Cross Street Gallery

The Main Cross Street Gallery of fine art, 218 Third Ave. N. is located on the grounds of the beautiful Bullock-Martin House, which was built around 1887. It is a classic example of late Victorian architecture and is a significant contribution to the Franklin historic district. Illustrating the practicality of preserving and fully utilizing historic structures, owner Heather Martin and husband Eddie both live and work in the house. The gallery office is located in the front parlor of the home, while the art occupies the loft of a charming period cottage behind the house, as well as the home's lush garden.

The gallery boasts of a variety of traditional fine oil paintings and sculptures by nationally-recognized contemporary artists. You'll find European and American scenes, landscapes, still life and floral paintings, and inspirational and religious works.

There is a charming saying, "People choose new homes, but historic homes choose people." Heather and Eddie Martin believe that this home did in a way "choose" them. They were familiar with the historic house because it had been the studio and art gallery of their family portrait photographer, Sam Causey. Mr. Causey had passed away that year, and most everything from the studio had been sold. However, when they went into the house to look at the property, they were amazed to see a copy of a portrait Sam had taken of the Martin family years earlier hanging right above the mantle!

Perhaps the house did "find" them, because the Martins have lovingly restored the home, and graciously share its charm with the community. It is open to the public for weddings and special events. For rental information and rates, contact Heather at 615-599-8298. The gallery is open Monday–Saturday 10 am-6 pm.

BAKERY - RESTAURANT

This beloved Franklin eatery at 110 4th Ave. S., has garnered praise from satisfied customers since 1984, and has been featured as a "favorite" by *Southern Living Magazine*. Merridee's owner Marilyn Kreider has applied her Mennonite baking skills to the well-known and loved recipes of the late Merridee McCray, and the result is absolutely delicious! Enjoy a heartwarming breakfast, a delicious lunch, or some coffee and a pastry, but don't leave without a loaf of Merridee's signature "Viking" five-grain bread. Open Monday–Saturday 7 am-5 pm. Catering and gift baskets are available. Call 615-790-3755.

Schakolad®
Chocolate Factory

If chocolate makes people happy, you'll be thrilled after visiting Schakolad Chocolate Factory at 443 Cool Springs Blvd. #107 in Franklin. All chocolates are hand-made and stacked in beautiful mounds in the display cases. Award-winning raspberry, Key Lime, Grand Marnier, and Italian Amaretto truffles are our favorites. The Schakolad (pronounced shaq-oh-LAD) Chocolate Factory is open Monday–Saturday 10 am-7 pm. Call 615-771-5077 or visit www.schakolad.com online.

Magnolia House Bed & Breakfast

A beautiful, ancient magnolia tree shades the covered front porch, lending its sweet, lemon-lime fragrance as well as its name to this special place. The Magnolia  House Bed and Breakfast at 1317 Columbia Ave. is nestled just outside of downtown Franklin on the site of the famous Civil War "Battle of Franklin." Four guestrooms are furnished with antiques and fine linens, each with its own bath. The rooms surround a spacious sitting room with a fireplace, books, magazines, games, and refreshments. Owners Robbie and Jimmy Smithson are delightful hosts who love having guests in their beautiful home.

A full-seated true "Southern style" breakfast is served every morning in the formal dining room or in the breakfast nook, and freshly brewed coffee is ready by 7 am for early risers. For more information or reservations, call 615-794-8178 or visit www.bbonline.com/TN/magnolia.com.

Children's

For the best selection of children's clothing in Central Tennessee, visit The Little Cottage in Franklin. Owned by a mother and her two daughters, they know what you are looking for when clothing children. This incredible boutique carries specialty items such as smocked dresses in batiste and silk, lovely christening gowns, and coordinated traditional outfits at moderate prices. For the aspiring dancer in your life, browse through the new dance attire section. The Little Cottage offers a baby registry and personal shopping services for your convenience. For that special gift, choose among sterling silver rattles and cups or fun portrait wear. The Little Cottage, 230 Franklin Rd., is part of The Factory—a former stove factory renovated for one-of-a-kind retail shops. Visit Monday–Thursday 9:30 am-5 pm, Friday 9:30 am-6 pm, Saturday 10 am-6 pm and Sunday noon-5 pm. Call 615-794-1405.

UNIQUE GIFTS FOR BABY

Visit the Plaid Rabbit—Angie Patterson's fabulous baby boutique—to buy something special for that special baby in your life. More like the upscale shops you would find in Los Angeles or Manhattan, the Plaid Rabbit has all of the best in baby furniture; bedding and accessories; shower gifts; art; rugs; changing tables; clothing; and more! It is located at 443 Cool Springs Blvd. in Franklin and is open Monday-Thursday 10 am-5: 30 pm and until 6 pm Friday-Saturday. Call 615-771-9948.

FOR EVERY CHILD

Absolutely everyone will love this bright and beautiful store, from tiny tots and pre-teens, to new moms and grandmoms. There is truly something wonderful "for every child" tucked into every corner of this fabulous children's store at 111 Fifth Ave. N. in Franklin. Customers tell us it is "the most fun place to shop" for children's fashions, accessories, gifts, and home décor. Owner Dale Knight is proud to carry lines such as Baby Lulu—beautiful fabrics and styles; Zutano—bright mix and match colors for babies; Hartstrings and Kitestrings; and Groovy Girls dolls, furniture, and clothing. You will find things here you can't find in large department stores, like the special dressy coats by Rothschild. We were amazed at the vast selection of beautiful christening dresses for girls and boys, as well as First Communion dresses, flower girl dresses, and wonderful Halloween costumes! From great clothing and fun accessories to unique things for the playroom, we loved shopping in this exciting children's boutique. Open Monday-Saturday 9:30 am-5:30 pm and Sunday 1-5pm. Call 615-790-6426. For Every Child is a grandmother's dream!

Playful, Lively & Bright

Do you love designer clothing, chic shoes and stylish accessories that can usually only be found in New York or L.A.? If so, Enjoué is for you. Owner Bethe Smith, a graduate of O'More School of Design, is a friend to fashion forward females.

Enjoué, located in The Factory at 230 Franklin Rd. in Franklin, is open 10 am-5 pm Monday-Thursday, 10 am-8 pm Friday-Saturday and by appointment only on Sunday. Call 615-599-8177 or visit www.enjoueboutique.com.

THE CELLAR

Janice Swartz opened her specialty ladies' clothing store in "the cellar" of a gift shop. Relocating to 324 Main St., she kept the cute name. Wonderful apparel lines including Russ Berens, Northern Isles, David Brooks, Sharon Young, and Fresh Produce Sportswear for adults and children, make The Cellar a Franklin favorite. In fact, The Cellar has been named one of *Southern Living Magazine's* "203 Favorite Unique Shops in 2003." Hours are Monday-Saturday from 9:30 am-5 pm; so stop by. Call 615-790-9803.

Circa Home Interiors LLC

Circa ... the little store full of big surprises. The merger of expensive taste and affordability! With more than 30 years experience, Circa owner Ronnie Shue will help you make your home a fabulous showplace.

Circa has the largest selection of home entertainment wall units in Middle Tennessee. You'll also find sofas, bedroom groups, dining sets, lamps, art and more! Circa imports many items directly from overseas. Their affordable prices and high style are known across the nation. In fact, half their sales are to customers in New York, California and Florida!

Circa Home Interiors is off Hwy. 31 (Franklin Rd.) at 1106 Harpeth Industrial Ct.—the first building on the right. Circa is open Tuesday–Friday 11 am-5:30 pm and Saturday 11 am-5 pm. Call toll free 888-399-0170, 615-599-0170, or browse the extensive website at www.circahome.com. *(Color photo featured in front section of this book.)*

After working in the film industry for 11 years, Rebecca Poole "came home" to sell beautiful furniture her father and his team of craftsmen have been making since the 1960s. Rebecca's American Made Furniture at 341 Main St. in Franklin, is a showcase and outlet for furniture built to last many lifetimes. The store also carries a wide selection of unique gifts. Open 10 am-5 pm Monday-Saturday. Call 615-595-2553 or visit online www.rebeccasfurniture.com.

Yarrow Acres

With almost too many treasures to describe, Yarrow Acres at 424 A Main St. in Franklin is a little piece of paradise for gardening enthusiasts. Every nook and cranny holds a unique treasure—garden accessories, vintage floral pictures, jewelry, herb plants, herbal topiaries, gardening books, beauty products, and Yarrow Acres' own gourmet foods. No wonder this shop was named #39 in *Southern Living Favorites*! Open 10 am-5 pm Monday–Saturday and noon-4 pm Sunday. Call 615-591-7090.

Gifts & Home Décor

The Faye Snodgrass Gallery

Fine Art, Collectibles, Unique Gifts

When visiting charming historic Franklin, there are two places you won't want to miss. The Faye Snodgrass Galleries located at 344 Main St. and 230 Franklin Rd. at The Factory. Both locations offer gifts for every age and all occasions. You will find a number of lines exclusive to the area—and items made especially for The Galleries. The displays and the mix of merchandise make every trip a delightful outing. Faye and all of her employees are dedicated to making your visit a memorable one. Both locations offer complimentary gift-wrapping and are happy to ship your purchases. When visiting The Gallery at The Factory, be sure to stop by the coffee and tea bar. Your visit promises to be a memorable one! Visit the Main St. location Monday–Saturday 10 am-5 pm and Sunday 12:30-5 pm or call 615-591-7211. Visit The Factory location Monday-Saturday 10 am-5 pm or call 615-595-0833. Hours are extended during the holidays! *(Color photo featured in front section of this book.)*

GRAY'S
Card & Gift Shop

One of the oldest and most respected businesses in Franklin is this wonderful card and gift shop located right in the heart of downtown. It opened as Pope Drug Company in 1896, and was passed from partner to partner through the years, becoming Gray Drug Company in 1938. It carried that name until 1996 when the pharmacy was sold and Ralph Duke and daughter Laurie Gulan began its transformation into the great store it is today. Gray's Card & Gift Shop, 332 Main St., honors its history and the people of Franklin with the same wonderful customer service that made it so popular in the beginning.

Today, the shop is filled top to bottom with unique and exciting merchandise that Laurie is so proud to carry. There is a great selection of Thirsty Stone Coasters; Carlton Cards; Ty Beanie Babies; Windsport Garden Boppers and Windsocks; and unique frames, mugs and candles. One of the most unusual items in the store is the line of Tumbleweed Pottery—the perfect gift for someone with a sense of humor. The pretty jars are labeled with such clever names

as, "Blonde Moments," "Ashes of Problem Employees," "Harley Fund," "Little White Lies," and even "Boob Job Fund!" These are great to fill with your favorite candy, treats, and yes, money! The atmosphere of the store is very upbeat and happy, filled with great merchandise and customers' laughter.

Just look for the vintage neon sign at the door. It is one of the focal points of historic downtown Franklin. Gray's Card & Gift Shop is open Monday–Friday 10 am-5 pm and Saturday until 4 pm. Be sure to visit www.grayscardandgift.com online, or call 615-794-4595.

The Heirloom SHOP

Step through the doors of The Heirloom Shop at 404 Main St., and you'll feel as though you've walked into a treasure chest. The colorful Christmas items, gleaming serving pieces, painted glass, and brilliant jewelry make the entire store seem to "sparkle!" A draped archway creates a beautiful entrance into the magical store, which is filled with treasures from Dept. 56, Christopher Radko, Arthur Court, Byers Choice Carolers, and a great selection of decorative accessories for the home.

Owner Rose Wright with her daughter/partner, Jerrie Martin and their merry helpers are just the nicest ladies you will ever meet. Together, they bring joy and excitement to historic downtown Franklin. Every item here is sure to become a treasured "heirloom" for generations to come. The store is open Monday-Saturday 9:30 am-5 pm and Sunday 1-4 pm. Call 615-791-0110.

CHERIE'S UNIQUE COLLECTION

Nestled in The Factory at Franklin, Cherie's Unique Collection contains fascinating home accessories and jewelry from around the world. You'll find the best in scented candles, the famous Lampe Berger fragrant lamps from Paris and uniquely designed hand-blown glass and wine racks and much, much more.

Proprietor Cherie Dukas takes pride in stocking elegant, distinctive and whimsical items individually selected by her from her travels around the world—Italy, France, Russia, and Germany to name a few. Here you'll find that perfect gift—especially that gift with a little attitude.

You won't want to miss Cherie's Unique Collection, located at 230 Franklin Rd. 11-J, 10 am-5 pm Monday–Thursday and 10 am-6 pm Friday-Saturday. Call 615-599-9904.

INN & SUITES

You'll be welcomed by a smile and treated like family at the Baymont Inn & Suites, 4207 Franklin Commons Ct. This beautiful inn is convenient to historic Civil War sites and antebellum homes, and is less than 3 miles from Franklin's historic downtown Main Street shopping. The rooms include large desks, speaker phones, outlets for laptops, cable TV, hair dryers, irons, and coffeemakers. Businessmen will appreciate the special corporate meeting rooms, as well as the indoor swimming pool and spa. In keeping with the best in "Southern hospitality," a delicious continental breakfast is served, which includes hot French toast and waffles. For reservations, visit www.baymontinns.com online or call 615-791-7700, or toll free 877-BAYMONT.

The freshly baked cookies at the end of the day are the perfect finishing touch to your remarkable stay at the Hampton Inn & Suites, 7141 South Springs Dr. This 127-room hotel is only a few miles from more than 25 well-known restaurants; adjacent to Cool Springs Galleria and Recreation World; three miles from the Legends Golf Club; and four miles from historic downtown Franklin. The staff is extremely friendly and helpful, with front desk service 24 hours a day. All suites are two separate rooms with a fully-equipped kitchen and king size bedroom; two telephone extensions; two televisions; and a living room sofa that converts to a bed. Business travelers will find a work area; direct-dial telephones; computer/fax hookups; voice mail; and available conference room that will accommodate up to 10 people. A flip chart easel; a dry erase board; a TV/VCR; a screen; and an overhead projector are available for an additional charge. Families will also appreciate the extra special touches, such as: TV with free HBO; in-room movies; coffee maker; hair dryer; iron and ironing board; and a guest laundry facility. There is dry cleaning Monday-Saturday, and a complimentary shuttle within a five-mile radius.

At the end of the day, enjoy the on-site exercise room and access to an off-site fitness center. A supermarket is nearby for grocery shopping, and a complimentary expanded continental breakfast is served from 6-10 am daily in the lobby. The Hampton Inn & Suites is the perfect place to headquarter for visits to Opryland and the Grand Ole Opry, as well as the Nashville Fairgrounds. Its great location, excellent personal service, and first-class accommodations make it a first choice for Tennessee travelers. For reservations, call 615-771-7225 or visit www.hamptoninn.com online.

Bone DuJour

Gourmet Pet Bakery

Shopping for your four-legged loved ones has never been easier or more fun than in this very cool pet boutique and gourmet bakery at 420 Cool Springs Blvd. #140 in Franklin. Owners Susan Blackwood and Sandi Brim have definitely solved the dogging problem of "What to buy for the mutt who has everything!" At Bone Du Jour, you can pick up everything from gourmet, tail-waggin, peanut butter bones to CD's of "Pet Tunes" for dogs, cats, and birds. The bakery is the biggest part of the business, offering something for every taste. You'll find Dog Giorno Pizza, Sushi for the Poochie, Cinnabone Rollovers, Nutty Puppies, Bacon/Cheddar-flavored bones, and Veggie Twists for the calorie-conscious canine. Seasonal cookies are a specialty, and believe it or not, you can even order a birthday cake or treats for your pet's Easter Basket and Valentine's Day gift.

Want something pretty and unique for Grover or Miss Kitty? How about a Swarovski crystal-inlaid leather collar or Burberry jacket, a luxury dog bed from So Sadie, or fancy hair accessories. You can even sample the line of designer colognes, which include *Pucci, Beautifur, Liz Claibone,* or *Tommy Holedigger*. Now if you think you have heard it all—you haven't. The piece de resistance, or so we thought, was the pendant with crystal initials your puppy-loving pet can present to his "amore." The store carries pet-related items for us two-legged creatures as well, such as picture frames, lamps, cell-phone covers, and figurines.

Store hours are Monday through Friday 10 am to 7 pm and Saturday 10 am to 6 pm. Call 615-503-9742 or visit www.bonedujour.com.

Restaurants

Capture the "Flavor of Franklin" at Sandy's Downtown Grille, 108 4th Ave. S. The dark brick exterior, gleaming hardwood floors, and lustrous mahogany furniture, create a sophisticated ambiance—perfect for romantic dinners, yet casual enough for "ladies on a day out." All menu items are prepared in-house from scratch, using only fresh, high-quality produce, meat, and seafood in a combination of both simple and complex tastes. Everything is delicious! Owner Sandy Ligon invites you to join him for lunch 11 am-2 pm, (until 4 pm Saturday) or dinner 5-9 pm, (until 10 pm Friday–Saturday). Visit www.sandysdowntowngrille.com online or call 615-794-3639.

One of the brightest new culinary "gems" in Franklin, Saffire at The Factory, 230 Franklin Rd., sparkles and shines with a big city flair, yet affords diners a chic, intimate atmosphere. The food is exciting—every plate creative enough to grace a magazine cover, and every single item is delicious! Restaurateur/caterer Tom Morales describes it as "comfort food with a culinary twist." For extraordinary dining—visit Saffire! Reservations recommended. Call 615-599-4995.

Antonio's Ristoranté Italiano is one of the best-kept secrets in Franklin. If you're looking for authentic Italian food, you'll find it here! Owners Frank and Annie Mariani are outstanding hosts in the wonderful, fun, and very popular "ristoranté Italiano," located at 119 Fifth Ave. N. You will love watching chef Annie cook your dinner in the great open kitchen in the center of the restaurant. We adored the unique creamy Polo Marsala and the Italian Stuffed Salmon. No wonder Antonio's was named a winner in the "2003 Nashville City Search" for best restaurants! Antonio's is open for lunch Monday-Friday 11 am-2 pm with dinner hours being Monday–Thursday 5-9 pm and Friday–Saturday until 10 pm. Reservations recommended. Stop by for fine dining with a relaxed and friendly atmosphere. Look for the corner building with the attractive green and white wrap-around awning. For more information, call 615-790-1733.

Don't miss Nashville Pizza Co., the perfect place for families to enjoy "the  best pizza in Franklin." Each pizza is made to order, the dough is hand-made daily, and the breadsticks, sandwiches and salads are prepared fresh too! Visit both Franklin locations: 2176 Hillsboro Rd. and 152 Watson Glen. Open for your dining in or carryout pleasure, Monday–Thursday 11 am-9 pm, until 10 pm Friday–Saturday. Call 615-591-7050 or 615-595-8001.

THE DAISY CHAIN

As fun and pretty as its name, The Daisy Chain, 330 Mayfield Dr., #C-8 (Carothers Corner Center) in Franklin, is probably the most wonderful "Girly Store" you will ever visit, and owner Courtenay Twinam Golden one of the most endearing women you'll ever meet. She makes absolutely no apologies to men for her totally "girly store" that is filled with unique and creative items appealing to the feminine, playful sides of ladies of all ages. From antiques and collectibles, to bath and body products and jewelry, to garden art and home décor, you will find a perfect gift for the special "girl" in your life—mother, daughter, sister, and friend. Customers say that they come in because they need "A Daisy Chain Fix." Once you experience The Daisy Chain, you'll understand why! Courtenay tries to make everyone feel welcome and wanted, "like an old friend coming by the house." Nostalgic music fills the air and sweet smells entice the senses. But, the real treat is the merchandise. Items are displayed by color, so that customers can visit the vignettes that "speak to them personally," and Courtenay works hard to find lines that are unique, fresh, affordable, and new—without being too trendy. You'll find antiques, collectibles, rustic garden art, gifts, watering cans, hand-blown glass hummingbird feeders, artist-designed birdbaths and planters, candles, vintage furniture, textiles and much more! With Courtenay's background as a graphic artist, she is able to help customers with creative ideas for their homes and gardens, as well as offer referral services such as upholstery, refinishing, and marble painting. We know you will love The Daisy Chain, open Tuesday–Friday 10 am–6 pm and Saturday until 5 pm. Call 615-771-0767.

Plum Delicious

Long before Linda Diamantas was selling English tea sets at her specialty foods gift shop, she and husband, Michael, were Felony Probation and Parole officers.

Since turning in her badge, Linda has taken up gift baskets and jams at her shop, Plum Delicious, 230 Franklin Rd., Building 11-AA. From gourmet foods and chocolates to Greenhills music and baby gifts, Plum Delicious has a gift or custom-made gift basket for any occasion.

For more information, call 615-595-7586. Open Monday–Thursday 10 am–5 pm and Friday–Saturday 10 am–6 pm.

SOUTHERN RHAPSODY, INC.

When Allen and Cynthia Guillory opened their beautiful 5,000-square-foot retail store in The Factory at Franklin in October 2003, it was to a preview crowd of awestruck people! Southern Rhapsody, "The Soul of Southern Style," 230 Franklin Rd. Bldg. 14, is a high-end retail store that showcases exquisite furniture, stunning accessories, gorgeous tabletop and decorative items, fine linens, unique accents, fabulous children's collectibles, and beautiful fine art. The essence of classic Southern design is in the details, and these details are evident throughout the beautiful showroom. Customers enjoy a complimentary café-style coffee and cappuccino bar and free gift-wrap, design and delivery services. The store is open Monday–Saturday 10 am-6 pm and Sunday 1-5 pm. Visit www.southernrhapsody.com online or call 615-595-1313 for more information. You, too, will be "awestruck!" *(Color photo featured in front section of this book.)*

Be sure and check out Bella Linea in Franklin at 335 Main St. See page 47 for full details.

Tearooms

This beautiful 1892 Victorian mansion in Franklin's historic district has been restored into one of the area's most prized treasures. Lillie Belle's of Franklin is as pretty and remarkable as the "ladies" she was named to honor. Owner Bud Carman's grandmother was Lillie Bell, Barbara Carman's grandmother was Lillie Mae, and the Corn family who owned the house for 60 years owned "Lily Flour Mill." It had to be "Lillie." There is a lot of history within this Queen Anne style home, located just off the square at 132 Third Ave. S., but today it is home to a wonderful tearoom and gift shop. You can make a reservation for a Victorian afternoon tea, or a delicious lunch. You'll enjoy shopping in the unique gift shop. You can "take your tea" on the beautiful Garden Porch where you'll enjoy the view of flowers and herbs, or in the Garden Room, which is filled with white wicker and the special touches that will remind you of Grandmother's house.

The lunch menu is a fabulous combination of seasonal salads, soups, sandwiches, quiche, fresh fruits and delicious desserts. For tea, choose from scones with Devon cream and preserves, soup, fruit, and finger sandwiches, and wonderful tea. Lillie Belle's features more than 15 loose teas and homemade Tea Cakes, all available for purchase. Stop by Tuesday–Saturday 11 am-2 pm for lunch or make reservations for a Victorian afternoon tea, 2:30-4 pm.

Also, Lillie Belle's has become a favorite place to have a wedding or reception. A charming garden gazebo is completely enclosed with brick and wrought iron, and the grounds are landscaped with flowers and fountains. The setting is lavish and romantic—perfect for the most memorable day in your life. Call 615-790-2300 or visit www.lilliebelles.net online. *(Color photo featured in front section of this book.)*

Wines & Wineries

A quality bottle of wine is the perfect addition to any occasion, and Walker's Wine & Spirits has just what you need! You'll especially love its selection from smaller wineries.

In addition to great wines, owner John Walker is committed to providing excellent service. "We try to care about each customer as an individual," he says.

John's family has lived in the Franklin area for more than 180 years, so he takes special pride in welcoming newcomers. "Educating people about wines and spirits," he notes, "helps to share the history of the area and maintain the sociability which was and is a major part of Southern culture."

Walker's Wine & Spirits, Inc., 330 Mayfield Dr., is open Monday–Wednesday 10 am-9 pm and Thursday–Saturday 9 am to 10 pm. Visit www.walkerswineandspirits.com online or call 615-778-7673.

DISCOVER GALLATIN/HENDERSONVILLE/ GOODLETTSVILLE

GALLATIN

Even though the town of Gallatin is just a short distance from large cities and major markets, it has succeeded in retaining that wonderful quaint atmosphere reminiscent of days gone by. The town is proud of its image, and it takes pride in its friendly people.

In The Beginning

Gallatin's history, like other communities in the area, began with the Mound Builders and Longhunters, but the first pioneer settlers were Henry Scaggs and Thomas Sharpe Spencer. When Tennessee became a state in 1796, special commissioners purchased land from Captain James Trousdale and laid out the town of Gallatin. It was named for Albert Gallatin, Secretary of the Treasury under President John Adams and President Thomas Jefferson.

Gallatin became one of eight Tennessee towns chosen to be a part of National History Preservation—a pilot program intended to revitalize downtown areas. Gallatin's downtown has indeed seen a re-birth—with business owners opening their doors with a faith in the people of the town . . . sort of a "if you build it, they will come" attitude. As a result, the downtown has managed to acquire a sense of real community, much as it experienced in the past. Many of the old and abandoned buildings have sprung to life, and they are becoming points of interest for visitors. One example is The Palace—the oldest silent movie theater still standing—which has been renovated into a community movie house.

The Trousdale Place on West Main Street is another Gallatin attraction. This stately, historic, two-story, brick house was built in 1813 by John H. Bowen and acquired by William Trousdale in 1822. Trousdale served in the Creek Indian War, the War of 1812 under Andrew Jackson, the Seminole War of 1836, and as a Brigadier General during the Mexican War. The home is open to visitors, and the grounds are available for weddings, receptions, and reunions.

History buffs won't want to miss a visit to the handsome log inn called Wynnewood, just seven miles east of Gallatin. It was erected in 1828 to serve as a stagecoach inn and mineral spring resort, and it's believed to be the largest log structure ever built in Tennessee. Some of the logs composing the walls are 32 feet long! It has been conveyed to the State of Tennessee for preservation as a historic site, and it's open to the public all year.

Gallatin is a people-oriented community, determined to grow and prosper; yet hoping to remain as serene and quaint as it is today. You will enjoy getting to know its history and becoming acquainted with the local business owners who are excited about the energy and growth of their city.

HENDERSONVILLE

If you are a history buff, you are in for a wonderful treat as you tour this interesting, beautiful Tennessee town. Archeologists have found artifacts dating back to the Ice Age, and the area has a rich history as a hunting ground for several Native American tribes. Hendersonville, Tennessee is located in Sumner County, just minutes from Nashville. Residents enjoy the quiet, peaceful, slow pace of life in a small, rural town, yet can easily take advantage of all that the "big city" has to offer.

Outdoor Beauty

One of the city's most beautiful assets is Old Hickory Lake on the Cumberland River, which is home to a wildlife viewing site. These recreation areas are complete with picnic and camping facilities, several lakeside parks and four marinas. Whether you enjoy fishing, picnicking, water skiing, jet skiing, camping or just lazy-day tube floating, Old Hickory has something for everyone.

As you cross Hendersonville's western border, you'll see the 140-year old mansion Monthaven, which serves as the home of the Hendersonville Arts Council. The council offers classes in visual arts, music and drama for adults and children. Its gift shop features pottery and woodcarvings by local artisans and craftsmen.

Things To Do And See

There are many fun fairs and festivals in Hendersonville throughout the year, but if you happen to be visiting during September, you'll enjoy Rock Castle's yearly fundraiser. This is a reenactment dedicated to the preservation of early Tennessean frontier history, bringing together Longhunters, trappers, traders, vendors, and entertainers with lots of fun and food for the entire family. Here you can take a tour of the first stone home built in Middle Tennessee. During the Christmas holiday season, enjoy the lighted boat parade along Drakes Creek hosted by the Junior Chamber of Commerce.

And, like all of the towns we have discovered in this beautiful and friendly part of Middle Tennessee, Hendersonville has fabulous shopping and bargain opportunities. We loved poking around in antique stores, tasting the country fare in the quaint eateries, and meeting some of the friendliest people in the world. You'll love it too!

GOODLETTSVILLE

Although Goodlettsville is one of five cities located within the Nashville city limits, it has managed to retain a delightful "small-town" charm. It was settled in 1779 by Kasper Mansker, and is one of the oldest settlements in the Middle Tennessee area. Its historic Main Street is a delightful mix of antique stores, specialty shops and family-owned restaurants, and exciting festivals and special events are planned throughout the year.

Family Fun And Shopping

You won't want to miss the Mansker's Station Frontier Life Center—a perfect day for the family. You can experience the lifestyle of early settlers and learn how they lived at this authentically reconstructed 1779 log station typical of the first settlement. You can hear the click of spinning wheels; smell the smoke from the cook fires; and imagine the rumblings of Goodlettsville's past. It is history come to life.

You will enjoy great shopping, great museums, family fun and recreation, sightseeing tours, and delicious Southern dining in Goodlettsville. The RiverGate Mall is one of Tennessee's largest shopping malls, with more than 150 stores and specialty shops, and a food court with more than a dozen restaurants. You'll find several great antique malls, which will keep you busy for hours, as well as garden shops, museums, and a Main Street Playhouse theater with a great schedule of entertainment.

For more information about Gallatin, contact the Gallatin Chamber of Commerce at 615-452-4000, or visit www.gallatintn.org online.

For additional information about Hendersonville, contact the Hendersonville Chamber of Commerce at www.hendersonvillechamber.com online or call 615-824-2818. You may also contact Sumner County Tourism at 615-230-8474, or visit www.sumnercountytourism.com online.

For more information about Goodlettsville, contact the Goodlettsville Chamber of Commerce at www.goodlettsvillechamber.com online or call 615-859-7979.

February
    Bluegrass Festival

April
    Squarefest
    Pilgrimage of Homes

July
    Independence Celebration

August
    Sumner County Fair

October
    Festival on Main
    Candlelight Cemetery Tour
    BBQ Cookoff

November
    Christmas Harvest Craft Fair

December
    Christmas Parade

Hendersonville Fairs Festivals & Fun

March
 Home and Garden Tour

April
 Pilgrimage of Homes
 Taste and Tunes of Hendersonville

May
 Crafts Fair at Monthaven
 Garden Tour

June
 Worth/Twitty ASA National Qualifying Tournament

July
 Independence Day Celebration
 Freedom Festival
 Jet Scream Personal Watercraft Competition

September
 General Daniel Smith Days & Fair

October
 Festival by the Lake

December
 Christmas Parade
 Christmas at Rock Castle
 Christmas on the Creek Lighted Boat Parade

Goodlettsville
Fairs Festivals & Fun

January
Long Hollow Jamboree (monthly)
Long Hollow Winery (monthly)
Main Street Playhouse (monthly)
Mansker's Station Saturday
  All-Day, Hands-On Workshops
  & Sunday Afternoon Programs
  (monthly)

February
Bridal Fair

March
Rook Tournament
Spring Encampment

April
Lawn and Garden Expo
Pilgrimage of Homes

May
Colonial Fair

June
Home & Garden Tour

July
4th of July Celebration and
  Living History Encampment
Tennessee/Kentucky
  Threshermen's Show
  (Springfield)

August
Sumner Crest Winery's Grape
  Stomp and Concert

September
Bowen-Campbell Auto Expo
Sumner Crest Winery's Classic
  Car Show and Free Concert
"SPIRIT" Play about legendary
  Bell Witch (Springfield)

October
Fall Encampment
Pumpkin Fest

November
Antique Festival
Sumner Crest Winery's
  Christmas Open House

December
"Lights Fantastic" Christmas
  Parade & Lighting of the Tree
Yulefest and Living History Camp
Hunters Lane High School Annual
  Christmas Crafts Fair

SPRINGFIELD ROBERTSON COUNTY
CHAMBER OF COMMERCE

Springfield, county seat of Robertson County, is as old as Tennessee itself, having been established in 1796. In recent years, the downtown area near the public square has developed into a delightful place for day-trips and weekend jaunts.

Major points of interest include the 135-year-old courthouse with its unique clock tower, many beautifully restored buildings and an excellent county museum housed in the old post office built in 1915. The county archives and Gorham-McBane Public Library are within easy walking distance of Main Street.

Several antique shops, bookstores, a movie theater, a tearoom, and other charming restaurants are downtown with many other retail choices within a few blocks. A new public greenway connects downtown with two beautiful city parks while other shopping opportunities and additional restaurants are within one mile of downtown.

Nearby Adams, 10 miles north on US 41, hosts the annual Tennessee/Kentucky Threshermen's Show each July and is the site of the play "SPIRIT" each fall, which tells the story of the legendary Bell Witch. The chamber is open Monday-Friday 8:30 am-4:30 pm, at 100 5th Ave. For more information, call 615-384-3800, or visit www.springfieldtennchamber.org online.

Photo by Gina Head

GOODLETTSVILLE ANTIQUE MALL

Two Lindas. Two best friends. Too many treasures to mention... Linda Marksberry and Linda Mahaffey have shared many things in life—vacations, homes, grandchildren, and a love for antiques. Today, they share a very successful business—the Goodlettsville Antique Mall. Stroll through 30,000 square feet of antiques and see yesterday's memories, today! Discover furnishings from primitive to English, glassware from hard-to-find Depression glass to sparkling crystal, and goods in tin, stone and much more. Future plans are in motion to include a coffee shop where you can break from shopping and enjoy a fresh cup of coffee or maybe split a yummy dessert. The Goodlettsville Antique Mall is conveniently located at 213 N. Main St. in historic Goodlettsville. Open Monday-Saturday 9 am-5:30 pm and Sunday 11 am-5:30 pm. For more information, visit www.goodlettsvilleantiquemall.com or call 615-859-7002.

ANTIQUES ON MAIN

All of the folks at Antiques on Main are friendly and they love antiques. This 10,000-square-foot building is located at 117 W. Main St. in downtown Gallatin among other unique businesses, old churches, and restored buildings. Period streetlights highlight sidewalks and streets, creating a delightful atmosphere. Antiques on Main is a multi-dealer mall featuring many vendors. Merchandise is displayed in every inch of the building, and it's beautifully showcased in quaint room vignettes. Whether you collect a certain china, crystal, or silver, or simply love period furniture and art—you will find exactly what you want here! We found vintage clothing, estate jewelry, antique books, and hard to find collectible glassware. The mall is open Monday–Saturday 9 am-5 pm and Sunday 1-5 pm. Call 615-451-0426. Allow lots of time to visit Antiques on Main, because there is truly so much to see!

"Thanks to the Interstate Highway System, it is now possible to travel from coast to coast without seeing anything."

– Charles Kuralt

"Thanks to A Lady's Day Out, it is now possible to travel and see everything."

Art & Framing

Melanie's
Custom Framing

People come to Melanie Ashworth for all of their framing needs, but they also come for so much more. You will get the sense of this store's charm from Melanie and her long-time employee Jo Carver—their friendly personalities are legendary in Gallatin. Melanie's Custom Framing is located in a charming cottage at 435 E. Main St., complete with a front porch swing and colorful flowers. You'll also find unique gifts for everyone. Open Monday-Saturday 9 am-5 pm. Call 615-452-6227.

"Best Burger In Town!"
BLUE GOOSE CAFE

It is the oldest restaurant in Hendersonville, and it is one of Tennesse's favorites. The Blue Goose Café, 689 W. Main St. is the kind of warm and cozy place where you know you'll be served delicious home cooking and friendly country hospitality. The customers consist of lunching ladies to country music stars, construction workers to business people. You might even see regulars Joe Nichols, Marty Stewart or Lorrie Morgan sitting at the next table. The huge open kitchen, large windows and attractive décor are inviting and welcoming, but it is the delicious food that keeps everyone coming back again and again. Be sure to try their homemade burgers and the "Blue Goose Omelet." Open Monday-Friday 6 am-2 pm, and Saturday 6 am-noon. For information, call 615-822-8250.

Roxanna's

What a boutique! When Roxanna Polk says, "Boutique of Distinction," she means it. What began in 1989 as a small consignment shop featuring designer clothing has grown into the largest consignment shop in the Gallatin area. It not only offers wonderful bargains on women's and children's clothing but also has new and unique home accessories, gifts, gourmet foods, a huge assortment of jewelry, and hundreds of formal dresses. Roxanna's  even has a specialty "Grandma's Corner" with only the finest for those precious grandbabies. It is a must-see on your "Lady's Day Out." From baby to grandma, there is truly something wonderful for everyone. The second weekend in November is always the annual Christmas Open House, which is a special time for locals and visitors alike. You won't want to miss it! Visit Roxanna's 100 S. Westland Ave., Monday–Saturday 10 am-5 pm. For more information, call 615-452-4416.

Patricia Jane & Company

Shoppers, rejoice! You will absolutely love the remarkable Patricia Jane & Co. at 149 Bonita Pkwy. Owners, Patricia Rudy Woods, Tricia Caroline Woods, daughter, and Jane Greenway, aunt and Interior Designer, are from a well-known Nashville business family—Rudy's Farm Sausage. The beautiful old Hendersonville home has been transformed into an extraordinary setting featuring "theme rooms" that display furniture, lamps, rugs, art, pottery, crystal, baby and children's clothing, gourmet food items, cards, and candles. We also loved the iron-gated garden center, filled with unique garden treasures. It's a wonderful store, with fabulous finds! Patricia Jane & Co. is open Monday–Saturday 10 am-5 pm. Call 615-264-2377, toll free 866-PATRICIA, or visit www.patriciajaneandcompany.com online.

The Gossett House

Featuring

Occasions

Jaska Russell, along with family and friends, has transformed Portland's historic "Gossett House" into an incredible cache of beautiful and unique items for the home and added a restaurant and a tearoom with a delightful twist. A visit to **Occasions**, 103 W. McGlothlin St. will be a memorable "occasion" in itself! The front room is filled with a collection of the beautiful Vera Bradley purses and pocketbooks and wonderful sterling silver jewelry. Reproduction furniture displays Arthur Court pewter, sparkling crystal and unique tabletop décor. In the adorable kitchen, you'll find cookbooks, dishtowels, unusual kitchen gadgets, potpourri, pottery, and the popular Tyler candles.

Grandmothers love the upstairs rooms, which are filled with treasures for little girls and boys, and the entire house is decorated with remarkable framed art pieces. Occasions is open Monday–Friday 10 am to 5 pm and Saturday 9:30 am to 4 pm.

The restaurant **5 Chefs** is located in the back of the home in a beautiful addition that is absolutely perfect for garden parties, birthdays, bridal luncheons or coffee and dessert with friends. Beautiful landscaping, lanterns, water fountains and a gazebo provide a peaceful setting for special occasions. The restaurant is unique in that every day there is a different chef, and the menu varies according to that chef's imagination.

5 Chefs is open Monday–Friday 6:30 am to 4 pm. The Tearoom is available on Saturdays 10 am to 2 pm, reservations recommended. For more information call 615-325-9500.

Burdett's Tea Shop

&

Trading Company, LLC.

Burdett's Tea Shop, 618 S. Main in Springfield's antique district, is reminiscent of teashops in the UK, serving homemade scones, quiche, sandwiches and afternoon tea. Open Monday through Thursday 10:30 am to 2:30 pm and Friday through Saturday until 4:30. Call 615-384-2320 or visit www.burdettsteashop.com online.

Custom Creations

Love unique, specialized home décor? Then you'll adore Custom Creations! Owner Terry Kemper can create whatever you dream—draperies, bedding, floral designs, and more. Find your "Custom Creation" at 247 W. Main St., Ste. M in Hendersonville. Open Tuesday-Thursday 10 am-5 pm, Friday-Saturday 10 am-4 pm. To find out more, call 615-822-6753.

"A perfect stay every time"—that's Jameson Inn's guarantee. This inn will take your breath away—complete with a Southern plantation setting, large white columns, and welcoming hospitality. Each morning you'll enjoy a continental breakfast with homemade Belgian waffles. And, you can work off those calories in the fitness center and swimming pool. You'll find Jameson Inn at 1001 Village Green Crossing in Gallatin. Call 615-451-4494 or visit www.jamesoninns.com online.

Providing comfort and convenience at affordable prices is what Baymont Inn & Suites does best. During your stay, you'll enjoy the comforts of home and then some! Each room comes equipped with coffee makers, complimentary bottled water, pillow top mattresses and Down Lite pillows, ensuring that you will be refreshed and relaxed during your day. Non-smokers and those with disabilities will also find rooms just for them. Other amenities include free local calls, free voice mail, complimentary copies of USA Today, an outdoor pool, and a complimentary continental breakfast with waffles and French toast. With a staff that is eager to please, you'll receive superior service with a Tennessee smile.

Baymont Inn & Suites, 120 Cartwright St. in Goodlettsville, is open 24 hours a day, seven days a week. Call 615-851-1891, 877-BAYMONT, or visit www.baymontinns.com online. *(Color picture featured in front of book.)*

Bodyworks Emporium

Day Spa • Gift Store • Mind Spa

Entertainers Lorrie Morgan, Joe Diffie, and Billy Ray Cyrus call Bodyworks Emporium, 311 W. Main St. in Hendersonville, one of their favorite places to visit and shop. It's no wonder "Best of Nashville 2003" named it one of the top three places to get a massage. Owner Carolyn Greene and her staff of 13 offer the best in rejuvenating therapy and spa treatments. Open Monday-Friday 10 am-8 pm and Saturday 9 am-5:30 pm. Call 615-264-1111 or visit www.bodyworksemporium.com online. *(Color picture featured in front of book.)*

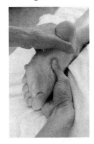

Memory Lane Scrapbooking

Rosie's love of pictures and scrapbooking led her to open this wonderful, fun, and very successful scrapbooking store at 835 Nashville Pike. After making "memory books" for others in Gallatin for many years, she now helps people learn the art of preserving memories through scrapbooking classes. Rosie carries a large selection of wonderful books and supplies such as the popular K&CO. Children's scrapbooking classes are also available. Call 615-230-5150 for information, or stop by for schedule.

Perkins Drugs & Gift Shoppe

Perkins Drugs & Gift Shoppe, 532 Hartsville Pike, has survived the Depression, two World Wars, and even "managed care" to make it to its 109th birthday in 2004. Owners Sam Rickman and Ferrell Haile have combined personal prescription care and counseling with an outstanding gift and bridal department, making Perkins Drugs a Gallatin favorite. Hours are Monday-Friday 8 am-7 pm, Saturday until 4 pm, and Sunday 1-4 pm. Visit www.perkinsdrugs.com online or call 615-452-6111.

 Be sure and check out Bedroom Elegance in Hendersonville at 387-A W. Main St. See page 46 for full details.

DISCOVER LAWRENCEBURG

Remember matching the famous quote with the famous person in Junior High School? One of those famous quotes was "Don't Give Up The Ship." Remember who said it? It was Captain James Lawrence, a famous hero of the War of 1812. This beautiful Tennessee town was named in honor of Captain Lawrence, and was first settled in 1815 along the Big Buffalo River. Lawrenceburg is the county seat of Lawrence County, and it has a great wealth of historical background. For instance, one of the first trails through the county was known as Military Road, once surveyed by Andrew Jackson and originally called Jackson Hwy. This road, which is known today as U.S. Hwy. 43, was a main thoroughfare during the Civil War by both the Union and Confederate soldiers.

King Of The Wild Frontier

History buffs know that one of the most famous figures in United States history hails from Lawrence County. The famous hunter, frontiersman, soldier, legislator, statesman, and hero of the Alamo— Colonel David Crockett—used to call Lawrenceburg home. David Crockett was born in the little community of Limestone in 1786 and moved to Lawrenceburg in 1817 to serve as Justice of the Peace. He helped establish a powdermill, a gristmill, and a distillery, but all were washed away during the Flood of 1821. David Crockett's small cabin is located 1 1/2 blocks south of the town's public square and is open for tours. Here you'll see memorabilia and pictures of his life, scrapbooks, and displays of clothing. A life-size bronze statue of Colonel Crockett stands on the south side of the square, welcoming all friends and visitors. Inscribed on the pedestal are his simple words, "Be sure you are right, then go ahead."

The beautiful David Crockett State Park in Lawrenceburg is a tribute to this American hero, and offers visitors unlimited recreational facilities. There are two campgrounds with modern bathrooms, biking trails, fishing areas, tennis and volleyball courts, and softball fields. If you are visiting during the month of August, you'll get the chance to be part of "Crockett Days"— one of the town's most anticipated events.

A Step Back In Time

The people of Lawrenceburg boast of many beautiful and unique points of interest, but they feel that their greatest resource is their people. This includes the community of the gentle Amish who settled in Lawrenceburg in 1944. Today, there are approximately 100 Amish families in the Lawrence County area. Their religion is the basis for their being, and they hold fast to three great values; a devout religion, a love of the land, and a close-knit family and community. Although they prefer to associate only with their own people, they are good neighbors, who have greatly improved the land in the Lawrence County area. All of their farming is done by hand, without the aid of tractors or modern equipment, and no electricity is used anywhere in their community. This has been their way for more than 300 years. The Amish do not believe in bearing arms or taking oaths. Instead, they spend their lives following the peaceful examples of Christ. Visitors are welcome in their community, but please do not take pictures. You will be able to find the most interesting and unique handmade, priceless items throughout the Amish countryside, including homemade quilts, tack and harness, furniture, baskets, and candles. You will enjoy this experience and feel that you have indeed "stepped back in time."

Savor The Sights And Events

Nature enthusiasts will love the opportunities here in Lawrence County. It would be hard to find a more exciting adventure than a canoe ride on Shoal Creek, one of Tennessee's leading tributaries. The pristine lakes and streams make the area a fisherman's paradise, and hunters from all across the South head to Lawrenceburg to find deer, turkey and dove. Golfers can choose from three unique golf courses, and race car lovers will enjoy the various classes of drag racing and dirt track racing.

Be sure to visit the Old Jail Museum, which houses many artifacts of Lawrenceburg history. You won't want to miss the Saint

Joseph Catholic Church built in 1872 or the James D. Vaughan Museum, which honors the founder of Southern Gospel Music. The two-night James D. Vaughan Festival features top gospel quartets, and attracts gospel music lovers from throughout the country.

And, of course, be sure to visit the Public Square and the beautiful countryside to find the many wonderful shopping and dining opportunities. The town advertises Lawrenceburg as, "A Beautiful Place to See, A Wonderful Place to Be!" It certainly is! We have to agree!

For additional information about Lawrenceburg, contact the Lawrenceburg Chamber of Commerce online at www.chamberofcommerce.lawrence.tn.us or call 931-762-4911.

COLUMBIA

MAURY ALLIANCE

Whether you are shopping for fine clothing, or scouring the shops for timeless antiques, you'll find it in Columbia's delightful downtown district. Enjoy a relaxing lunch at one of the square's unique eateries while you decide which of the many specialty stores you'll visit next. While the citizens of Columbia and Maury County look to the future with great enthusiasm, the past has been preserved and respected through its wonderful museums and city festivals. If you are visiting during April, you can help celebrate "Mule Days," or take part in "Mule du Gras" during May. "Jazz in June" brings the town square to life, and you can step back into the day of poodle skirts and milkshakes during "Cruisin the Square" in July. For more information, call 800-205-9641, 931-388-2155, or visit www.mauryalliance.com online. Maury Alliance office hours are 8 am-5 pm Monday-Thursday and 8 am-4:30 pm Friday.

Lawrenceburg Fairs Festivals & Fun

January
    Tennessee Valley Jamboree (monthly)

June
    Summertown Bluegrass Reunion
    Heritage Festival

July
    Loretto Fourth of July Picnic
    James Vaughan Festival

August
    David Crockett Days
    Summertown Bluegrass Reunion

September
    Middle Tennessee District Fair

October
    Loretto OktoberFest
    Mt. Zion Sugar Creek Festival

November
    Christmas in the Country

December
    Lawrenceburg Christmas Parade
    Christmas Pops

HOLLAND'S DRUG

This family-owned, old-fashioned pharmacy and gift shop has been a Lawrenceburg tradition for more than 40 years. Holland's Drug, Inc., located at 11 Public Sq. in the beautiful historic downtown area, is just as you imagine it would be. You'll find pharmacy needs, special Hallmark cards, baby and wedding gifts, and the wonderful Holland family, who know their customers by name! The store is open Monday-Saturday 8 am-7 pm. Call 931-762-5551.

Richland Inns

This locally owned, two-story hotel has a warm, cozy, "hometown" atmosphere, and it's within walking distance of great restaurants, shopping, and a movie theater. The Richland Inn, 2125 N. Locust Ave. in Lawrenceburg, offers suites and inside rooms with microwaves, refrigerators, hair dryers, irons, ironing boards, and coffee makers. And, some have Jacuzzi tubs! Enjoy a complimentary USA Today and continental breakfast each morning. Call 931-762-0061 for reservations.

Hampton Inn

This outstanding Hampton Inn at 1551 Halifax Dr. in Columbia is proud to have been recognized as being in the top five percent of all Hampton Inns in quality and service, and voted one of the top 20 out of the 1,000 best overall hotels! A delicious continental breakfast is served each morning, and business travelers will appreciate the high-speed Internet access. You'll find the friendly staff to be very helpful. Call 931-540-1222, 800-HAMPTON or visit www.hamptoninn.com.

The Brass Lantern

ROADHOUSE GRILL

The Brass Lantern represents local legendary people from the past to the present, as well as the historical places in which they have passed. Owner Johnny Fleeman features great Southern traditions with a flare! Be sure to visit The Brass Lantern, 2290 Pulaski Hwy. E. in Lawrenceburg or visit Legends Restaurant, 1609 N. Main St. in Shelbyville. And, be sure to pick up a bottle of Johnny's gourmet sauces or dressings to enjoy at home. To learn more, call 931-762-8134 or 931-762-0474.

Taste of the Town

A 1950s jukebox spins 45-RPM records from yesteryear, and the historical pictures throughout this popular Lawrenceburg restaurant enhance the nostalgic atmosphere. Today, Taste of the Town Restaurant, 204 E. Gaines, is filled with the smells of homemade dishes like Chicken and Dumplings, Chicken Fried Steak, and fresh fruit pies. The coffee is always on and the food is delicious! Open Monday-Saturday 6 am-7 pm. For more information, call 931-766-8132.

A neon "Roadrunner" greets customers at the front door of Chaparral's Steak House, 2475 Hwy. 43 N. in Lawrenceburg. The name was taken from the movie "High Noon," and the inside of the restaurant resembles the Old West. Chaparral's Steak House has become a local and tourist favorite. Try the ribeye, the grilled shrimp, or the Southern fried catfish. Open Monday through Thursday and Sunday 11 am-9 pm and Friday through Saturday until 10 pm. Call 931-829-1644 for all your catering needs.

Be sure and check out House~Blend in Columbia at 420 W. 7th St. See page 154 for full details.

DISCOVER
LEBANON

This charming Tennessee town has been nicknamed, "Antique City of the South." It's easy to see why! There are more than 20 antique stores in the area, as well as flea markets and large antique malls. Its small Town Square sports colorful awnings over the storefronts, beautiful pots of flowers, and friendly business owners. Stroll from one delightful shop to the next, or enjoy lunch or dinner at one of the great cafes or restaurants. You'll find everything from fast food to elegant cuisine.

The rich history of Wilson County is told through wonderful exhibits at the Wilson County Fairgrounds. Here you can visit a replica of the historic village called "Fiddler's Grove" with more than 30 restored historic buildings.

If the men in your group desire "high-octane" entertainment, then get them to the Nashville Speedway in Lebanon. All NASCAR enthusiasts will enjoy this stop. Visitors can actually ride or drive around the speedway in a real race car! So, appease your man with a NASCAR adventure, and then he might not mind shopping all the antique stores with you!

For additional information about Lebanon, contact the Lebanon-Wilson County, Tennessee Chamber at www.lebanonwilsontnchamber.org online or call 615-444-5503. You may also contact the City of Lebanon at 615-443-2839 or the Wilson County Convention and Visitors Bureau at 800-789-1327, 615-453-9655, or visit www.wilsoncountycvb.com online.

Lebanon
Fairs Festivals & Fun

March
    10K Checkered Flag Run/Walk

April
    Busch Race

May
    AARP Golf Tournament
    Antique Car Show
    Iris Show
    Wine Festival

June
    Bluegrass Festival
    Busch Race
    Civil War Re-enactment
    Phoenix Ball

July
    July 4th Celebration and Parade
    Dr. Cary Harbrecht Memorial Golf Tournament
    Indy Race

August
    Wilson County Fair
    Craftman Truck Race

November
    Car and Truck Show

December
    Festival of Lights
    Holiday Square
    Lebanon Christmas Parade

Wilson County

Convention and Visitors Bureau

Wilson County is close to everything and far from ordinary. Enjoy antique shops, historical sites, fun recreation and shopping opportunities in Lebanon, Mount Juliet and Watertown. Contact the Convention and Visitors Bureau Monday-Friday 8 am-5 pm at 800-789-1327, 615-453-9655 or visit www.wilsoncountycvb.com.

Near Everything...
Far from Ordinary!

CUZ'S ANTIQUE CENTER, 140 Public Sq. in Lebanon, not only features three buildings full of antique furniture, glassware and Middle Ages' architectural pieces, it is the home of the Fight'n Rooster Cutlery Co. too! Visit Frank Buster and staff Monday-Saturday 9 am-5 pm and Sunday 1-5 pm. Call 615-444-8070.

Town Creek Antiques is a family-owned-and-operated antique mall with more than 8,000-square-feet. Don't miss its large collection of vintage quilts, new and old Fenton lamps, and other Fenton collectibles.

Town Creek Antiques, 101 Short St. in Lebanon, is open Monday-Saturday 10 am-5 pm and 1-5 pm on Sunday. Call 615-453-9552 or visit www.towncreekantiques.com online.

Southern Rose Antiques

You will love browsing this wonderful antique store at 105 Public Sq. in Lebanon. The 81,000-square-foot building is filled top to bottom with wonderful Victorian antiques and collectibles. Open Monday-Saturday 10 am-5 pm. Enjoy the great lay-a-way plan! Call 615-444-3308.

THE HISTORIC INN AT:
CEDARVINE MANOR
A PREMIERE EVENTS FACILITY
Circa 1832

It has been recognized as one of the top three Tennessee Bed & Breakfasts by *The Tennessee Magazine,* voted "Best B & B" and "Best Place to Get Married" by Lebanon/ Wilson County Chamber, and featured on the PBS special "Tennessee Crossroads." Cedarvine Manor, 8061 Murfreeesboro Rd., east of Nashville, is one of the state's most historic inns and a premier events facility. The magnificent two-story home was built during the early 1800s, and after the Civil War it was used as a home for the war veterans. After a four-year renovation project, the incredible 8,000-square-foot manor and the 24-acre estate has been transformed into a spectacular inn and conference center. Eight guestrooms have a special decorative scheme, their own private bath, and include a hearty Southern-style breakfast each morning.

You'll also find an authentic 1832 log cabin/guest house, a formal courtyard with fountains, and a pond full of turtles on this lovely estate! Cedarvine Manor can accommodate large groups for reunions, retreats, weddings, receptions, or fundraisers. The Vine Center was rebuilt on the site of the original barn, and with its main dining room and full-service catering, it is perfect for large events. The Wild Vine BBQ Pavilion on the property can seat up to 400 guests for a large Tennessee shindig, and is complete with a locomotive BBQ grill. Cedarvine Manor is a breathtaking holiday party place, complete with thousands of lights illuminating the estate.

For more information, call 800-447-9155 or 615-443-2211. Visit www.CedarvineManor.com to see why Cedarvine Manor is considered to be Middle Tennessee's most outstanding "Historic Inn and Events Facility."

JUDY'S FASHION BOUTIQUE

Such a beautiful woman, such a beautiful story, and such a beautiful store! Judy Murphy began hand-painting women's and children's clothing and accessories to match when her children were young—darling mommy/daughter dresses, precious brother/sister outfits—all specially designed for each customer. Later, her 15 year-old son encouraged her to open her own fashion boutique, and thought it was the "greatest thing she had ever done." When her son was killed in an accident shortly after that, Judy used his passion as her inspiration to continue on, successfully building her business. Today, she still carries a great selection of clothing for "matching moms and children," as well as other wonderful well-known lines. Judy's Fashion Boutique is located at 307-B W. Main St. in Lebanon, and is open Monday-Wednesday 9 am-5 pm; Thursday-Friday until 6 pm; and Saturday 10 am-5 pm. Call 615-443-5433.

Florist, Gardens & Nurseries

MOSS'
Florist and Garden Center

Every lady's dream can be found at Moss' Florist & Garden Center. Award-winning designers are on hand to create exquisite fresh and permanent floral arrangements, as well as assist you in your garden and home décor needs. Would you like to plan and plant that perfect garden? Just ask one of the many horticulture experts for advice.

The Moss family began the business in 1952 as a feed and grain store. Today, it's much more. Choose from numerous framed prints and paintings, or place a custom framing order. The spacious showroom and greenhouses are conveniently located at 12110 Lebanon Rd. in Mt. Juliet. The Moss Family welcomes you with a friendly and fully-staffed facility. Hours are Monday-Friday 8 am-5:30 pm, Saturday 8 am-5 pm, and Sundays April-June and November-Christmas from 12:30-4 pm. For more information, call 615-758-5972.

Hotels

LEBANON/GOLD AWARD WINNER

A "preferred" hotel of the Nashville Superspeedway, Comfort Suites at 904 Murfreesboro Rd. in Lebanon offers deluxe suites; a grand lobby with fireplace; an indoor pool; a sauna; and a free breakfast buffet served each morning. Call 615-443-0027 or visit www.choicehotels.com/hotel/tn316.

SIGNATURE JEWELERS

Signature Jewelers of Lebanon is fast becoming one of the most talked about stores in the Nashville area. Owners Bridgette and Sonny Belew have the reputation as being "jewelers you can trust completely." The first thing you will notice when you visit this beautiful store is the 20-foot jewelers' viewing window! The bright, open space creates an inviting welcome to customers who want to sit at the coffee bar and watch the master designers at work. You'll be dazzled by endless showcases of some of the area's most beautiful and unique watches and jewelry. Bridgette Belew says, "We have no average customer here—our customers can get a $10 charm or a $10,000 diamond and receive the same quality of service for either purchase." Open Tuesday-Friday 9:30 am to 5:30 pm and Saturday 10 am-4 pm. Extended hours November-December. Shop online at www.signaturejewelers.com or call 615-449-9025.

Museums

CITY OF LEBANON MUSEUM & HISTORY CENTER

Walk through Lebanon's past and uncover the city's rich traditions. Discover the strides this quaint town has made since 1802. Visit the City of Lebanon Museum & History Center, 200 Castle Heights Ave. N., in the basement of City Hall. For more information, call 615-443-2839 or visit www.lebanontn.org.

Restaurants

Cafe 147

Café 147, housed in a historical landmark, invites its guests to stroll down Lebanon's memory lane through its collection of historic photographs. Nostalgic music, as well as scrumptious food await you at 147 Public Sq. in Lebanon. Visit Monday-Saturday 11 am-4 pm or call 615-443-4996.

You will feel as though you're in the cool canyons of the Southwest rather than in the smaller Tennessee town of Lebanon when you visit Mojave Rock Day Spa, 1670 W. Main St., #140. The serene, restful colors and uniquely soothing environment create a relaxing atmosphere to enjoy a day of pampering. Services include Dermalogica customized facials, medicated clearing treatments, Indian Sunset mud wraps, salt glow body polishes, and Parfango full body paraffin. Professional massage therapists offer Swedish, Neuromuscular, Craniosacral, Pre-Natal, Deep Tissue and Hot Stone massages. Also enjoy spa manicure and pedicure treatments as you never have before! Choose from several spa packages including "Mom's Day Out," "Boy's Day At the Spa" and the "Indian Package." It is open Monday-Thursday 10 am-7 pm, Friday 9 am-6 pm and Saturday 9 am-3 pm. Call 615-449-7880 or visit www.mojaverock.com.

JAMES E. WARD AGRICULTURAL CENTER / FIDDLERS GROVE

Encounter the late 1800s on each tour of Fiddlers Grove Historic Village. Nestled among the trees at the James E. Ward Agricultural Center, 945 E. Baddour Pkwy., Lebanon, you can stroll through 29 historic buildings. Tours are April-October, Tuesday-Friday 10 am-3 pm. Call 615-443-2626.

WILSON COUNTY FAIR

Voted "Champion of Champions Fair," the Wilson County Fair in Lebanon at the Ward Agricultural Center draws more than 350,000 people each August. Enjoy old-fashioned fun with music, shows, delicious regional

treats, and an exciting midway. Visit www.wilsoncounty.com/fair/ or call 615-443-2626.

Specialty Shops

Fine stationery, fabulous invitations, gorgeous silk albums, stylish gifts, Vera Bradley handbags and luggage—you'll always find something great at The Paper Mill, 126 Public Sq. in Lebanon. Open 8 am-5 pm Monday-Friday and 10 am-4 pm on Saturday. Contact owner Beth Winfree at 615-444-8399.

DISCOVER
LEIPERS FORK

Hospitality is something you can "hang your hat on" in the South, and this is particularly true of its sweet, small towns like Leipers Fork, Tennessee.

How It All Began

Before settlers arrived in this part of the country, Leipers Fork was a communal hunting ground to many prehistoric American Indians who later evolved into the tribes known today as the Shawnee, Chickasaw, and Cherokee. Thousands of historic relics dating back more than 4,000 years have been found in the rich fertile land. Although the land was rich and productive, the early settlers found the lifestyle harsh and untamed. It has been written that because of the unforgiving environment and frequent Indian attacks, it was a constant struggle just to till the land, feed the family, and reach old age with your hair on your head! Pioneering families from North Carolina settled the land around the late 1790s, given land grants as payment for their services in the Revolutionary War. Among the most famous settlers were the Bentons—Colonel Jesse Benton and his son Thomas Hart Benton—Thomas became a statesman and close friend to Andrew Jackson, and later a U.S. Missouri Senator. The town was first named Bentontown, and later changed to Hillsborough. It wasn't until 1818, when a post office was established in the village, that town leaders discovered there was already a town named Hillsborough, so the name of the village was changed again. It was named Leipers Fork in honor of the Leiper family who settled much of the land along the creek that passes through the village.

Leipers Fork is the only historic village on the Tennessee portion of the Natchez Trace parkway, and has become an area of choice for families wanting a rural atmosphere and the charm of country life. It is a Registered National Historic District, and it has kept its charming architecture characteristic of the Williamson County villages.

Stay Awhile

A favorite place of refuge and renewal for many notable citizens in the music industry, Leipers Fork might treat you to an impromptu outdoor performance by music notables. When country singer Naomi Judd mentioned "her town" (Leipers Fork) in a Travel Channel documentary about Nashville, visitors began to pour into the community to learn about this well-kept secret place. The atmosphere is as rustic as the art and antique stores dotting the countryside, and as down-home as the wonderful Southern meals served in the restaurants along the way. If you listen carefully on any Saturday night, you'll hear the ring of a banjo and fiddle echoing through the hills and hollows of the town.

Yes, time does seem to move slowly here . . . but that's OK. Take your time to explore the exciting shopping in Leipers Fork, and delight yourself in the charm of this rural historic village.

For more information about Leipers Fork, visit www.leipersfork.com online or call the Leipers Fork hotline at 615-595-8327.

Leipers Fork
Fairs Festivals & Fun

January
 County/Bluegrass Dance

February
 Ground Hog Eve
 Valentine Dance
 Puckett's After Hours (February-December)

April
 Beans & Blues
 Classic Movies (April-November)

May
 Country/Bluegrass Dance

June
 Computer Shoot

July
 Leipers Fork Bluegrass Festival

September
 Hillbilly Woodstock Costume Dance
 Tennessee Furniture & Art Show
 Chestnut Group Art Show

October
 Leipers Fork Woodcarving Show & Competition
 Leipers Fork Chili Cook-Off
 Halloween Trick or Treat

November
 Turkey Shoot
 Christmas Open House

December
 Christmas Open House
 Arts & Crafts Fair

Antiques

LEIPERS FORK ANTIQUES

Located in the heart of historic Leipers Fork in a 100-year-old country store, you'll find American country primitives in original surfaces, pottery, crock bowls, Griswold and Wagner cast iron, advertising signs, country store memorabilia and local art. Leipers Fork Antiques is also the "hangout" for area national recording artists, so you never know who might be in the picking corner on a Sunday afternoon.

Featured on the Travel Channel and the popular TV show "Tennessee Crossroads" for its unique history and charm, this store is a must see on your next visit to the Nashville area. Check out the corner office of the local historian where you'll see early pictures of the community or have lunch on the back porch deck overlooking the creek. Open Wednesday-Saturday 10 am-5pm and Sunday 1 pm-5 pm. For more information, contact Marty Hunt 615-790-9963.

DUMPSTER DIVERS ANTIQUES

Filled top to bottom with antiques and architectural salvage, Ted Fridholm's Dumpster Divers is not to be missed! You'll find mantles, stained glass and more! Visit Wednesday-Thursday 10 am-5 pm, Friday-Saturday 10 am-6 pm and Sunday noon-5 pm at 4154 Old Hillsboro Rd. in Leipers Fork. Call 615-591-3832.

LEIPERS FORK
FLINTLOCKS

As inspiration for his life's work, Greg Murry treasures this quote from a book written by his great, great, grandfather Victor Mouro Griswold: "All that we have is a gift from our divine Maker, and we must strive to bring glory to Him in all that we do." Greg's passion and talent as an engraver and arms maker have provided him with an age-old connection to the ancestors who inspired his calling as an artist. Visitors travel from all over the world to Leipers Fork Flintlocks, located at 4144 Old Hillsboro Rd. in Leipers Fork, to watch this master artist at work. He makes handcrafted Flintlock Rifles, which are his personal interpretations of elegant flintlock rifles from the 18th and 19th centuries. "Rifles such as these were an essential tool for our ancestors in the pursuit, creation, and preservation of freedom as we enjoy it today," Greg shares.

A gifted artist and craftsman, Greg is commissioned by customers to design and make rifles, pistols and tomahawks, executing every detail to the customer's personal taste. Engravings are "hammer-chased" in Old World fashion, with inlays of ivory, mother-of-pearl, silver and gold expertly incorporated into the wood. Some of the pieces take years to finish and all are museum quality masterpieces. His tools for making the rifles have changed very little in two centuries. However, Greg must create some of the tools himself. He uses fine chisels, mallets, files, engraving blades and jeweler's saws to make locks, screws, springs and triggers entirely by hand. Hours are Tuesday-Saturday 10 am-5 pm and Sunday 1-5 pm. Call 615-791-1747 or visit online at www.leipersforkflintlocks.com.

LEIPER'S CREEK GALLERY

Artist Lisa Fox has filled Leiper's Creek Gallery, 4144 Old Hillsboro Rd. in Leipers Fork, with impressive, vibrant fine art from local artists, many of whom are nationally and internationally recognized. For information, call 615-599-5102.

LEIPERS FORK ATTRACTIONS

Cabin at Leipers Fork

Natchez Trace

Surrounded by 140 acres of beautiful, rolling pastureland and bordered on one side by a trickling, peaceful stream, Leiper's Fork Bed and Breakfast is truly a slice of paradise. Look for the stone entrance and iron gate at 3340 Southhall Rd., in historic Leipers Fork. The beautiful home, which was built during the 1800s, still has many of the original architectural features including the wood floors, the staircase banister, and the authentic "slave wall," which surrounds the property. Each room is decorated according to its unique theme and furnished with Satellite TV, a DVD player, and a phone. A computer with Internet access is available in the library, and a beautiful music room features an upright piano, guitars, banjo and mandolins. To top off an incredible experience, you will enjoy a delicious gourmet breakfast served up with great Tennessee hospitality.

Leiper's Fork Bed and Breakfast is known for its magnificent surroundings and beautiful horse barns. If you are traveling with your own horses, you can board them on the property. Guests can swim in the heated pool, hike on the beautifully landscaped trails, or enjoy other outdoor activities such as archery, basketball or tennis. The many barns, gazebos, and spectacular structures on the property make this place perfect for weddings, receptions, reunions or other special events.

Your relaxation is the ultimate objective here, so you can do as little or as much as you desire. Nap in a hammock in the shade of the majestic oak trees, or venture into the village of Leipers Fork to the many antique stores, art galleries and restaurants. You will also find The Legends Golf Course just 15 miles away. For more information or reservations, call 615-794-9494, 866-LEIPERS or visit www.leipersforkbandb.com online.

Designer Glass

Dedicated to adding beauty and elegance to residential and commercial interiors in Nashville and surrounding areas, SGO Designer Glass specializes in what owners Martin and Lori Hilber refer to as "Stained Glass for the 21st Century."

SGO Designer Glass is a franchise of the world's largest artistic glass company. And, it's one of only 300 manufacturers worldwide that uses this unique process. Designer/Artist Lori Hilber works with clients to custom design art glass for their windows, cabinet doors, shower enclosures, grand entryways and skylights.

This showroom and manufacturing facility can be found in Leipers Fork in the Old Natchez House, which is listed on the National Register of Historic Places. Located at 4158 Old Hillsboro Rd., SGO Designer Glass is open Tuesday-Saturday 11 am-4 pm. For more information, visit www.leipersforkvillage.com online or call 615-790-7176.

VILLAGE GREENE BUILDING

Originally built in 1892, the Village Greene Building at 4150 Old Hillsboro Rd. in Leipers Fork still retains its original charm today. Various businesses call this home and invite you to visit. For more information, call 615-599-3676.

Williamson County has some of the richest farmland in Middle Tennessee, and no one knows the area better than the friendly folks at United Country Leipers Fork/The Oxford Company, 4151 Old Hillsboro Rd. in Leipers Fork. Their desire is to maintain the quaintness of the town as well as provide a service to long-time residents and folks moving into the area. They represent a multitude of owners with properties ranging from charming cottage bungalows to historic farms and plantations. With its 1880s design and period architectural elements—pine floors, architectural moldings, and stately antique staircase—the office building looks more like a beautiful historic tour home than a real estate office. For more information, call Cindy Garvey at 615-599-3676 or visit www.leipersfork.com.

DISCOVER
SAVANNAH/PICKWICK

Located in historic Hardin County, best known as the site of the pivotal Civil War Battle of Shiloh, the two tiny towns of Savannah and Pickwick offer visitors a glimpse into the life of the "true South." Hardin County is an area rich with history and blessed with a beauty that is legendary. Through the years, the citizens of the area have preserved the unique American history through nationally recognized museums, historic homes, and festivals that reflect the spirit of the region. When you are ready to "get away from it all," Hardin County, Tennessee is the perfect place to "get away TO it all!" Only two hours from Nashville, Hardin County provides a beautiful setting for boating, skiing, fishing, hunting, golfing, and many other recreational activities. The county is divided by the Tennessee River and Pickwick Lake, and much of its cultural importance is a result of the river. As you travel the rolling roads through the beautiful countryside, you will find reminders of the past at every turn, from the Shiloh National Military Park to the beautiful homes of historic Savannah. With its beautiful lakes, pristine streams and creeks, recreational opportunities, and progressive economic status, Hardin County has become one of the top ten retirement sites in America.

Great Fish Tales

World-class recreational facilities, incredible golf courses, and "tale-worthy" sport fishing lure visitors to this part of Tennessee for wonderful and memorable vacations. In fact, fishermen claim that the lakes and streams around Hardin County offer some of the best freshwater fishing in the world. Pickwick Lake is renown for its small mouth and large mouth bass fishing, which entices anglers from across the country. One "urban legend" claims that a catfish weighing in between 500 and 800 pounds was caught during the mid 1900s. In fact, locals will tell you about a picture of a man standing beside the monstrous fish, which lay on a wagon cart. This photo has sparked controversy for years, with some insisting it is fake and others fiercely defending it as the truth, protecting the county's reputation as "The Catfish Capital of the World." Real or not, it is a great fishing story! Be sure to ask about the National Catfish Derby, a six-week fishing rodeo and celebration, which was recently named as one of the nation's top 20 events.

Tee Time

If golf is your bag, you will find some of the most beautiful and most challenging courses in the world here in the rolling hills of Hardin County. The Shiloh Falls Golf Club, which was designed by Fred Couples and Jerry Pate, has received the Environmental Stewardship Award and the National Golf Foundation's Public Achievement Award. Every hole is "tree-lined" at the Pickwick Lake State Park Golf Course, which is a favorite of locals and visitors alike, and the Shiloh Golf Course (maybe Tennessee's best-kept secret) is a beautiful 18-hole course with a lot of historical significance. The cart path that connects the #2 green and the #4 green runs alongside the actual road that General Wallace used on his march into The Battle of Shiloh.

"Get Away To It All." To history-steeped hills and cemeteries that tell the stories of the Civil War, to the historic homes and museums that capture the spirit of the past, this area has it all. From the peaceful, crystal-clear waters and the fun they provide to the legendary golf courses and beautiful state parks—and, of course, the incredible shopping experiences—Savannah and Pickwick Lakes are rich with it all! Stop by soon!

SAVANNAH

Until 1830, Savannah was called "Rudd's Ferry," because James Rudd built a house on the riverbank and established a ferry. The ferry was later taken over by wealthy landowner and businessman David Robinson who built the beautiful historic Cherry

Mansion. According to folklore, it was Robinson's wife Sarah who named the town after her home city Savannah, Georgia. Of course the other, more colorful legend has it that a young girl named Anna fell into the water while boating, and someone yelled, "Save Anna!" The spot where she took her unexpected drenching was from that moment on called "Savannah." You decide!

As you tour the city of Savannah you will visit Cherry Mansion, which sits on the site of an Indian mound, high on a bluff overlooking the Tennessee River. The mansion is a Federalist-style home with 18-inch thick walls built of bricks, which were made right there on the river. During the war Cherry Mansion served as headquarters for General U.S. Grant just prior to the Battle of Shiloh. His tent was set up in the yard, but he slept in the house and took his meals with the Cherry family. Later, a field hospital was set up in the yard of the mansion, and hospital boats were moored below the house.

Simply Sensational

Even in her early days, Savannah was known as a very cultured, wealthy town—a great shipping center for freight and crossties. The Civil War did indeed take its toll on Savannah, but left her with a rich history that draws thousands of visitors each year. From its population of 800 in 1850, the town has grown today to only 7,500 people, so has been able to retain the appeal of a Southern home-town.

You will love touring the Savannah Historic District, the Savannah Historic Trail, the famous Trail of Tears, the Tennessee River Museum, and the wonderful refurbished downtown buildings which house exciting boutiques and specialty stores. Whatever you do, don't leave Savannah without a plate of crisp-fried catfish. After all, Savannah is known as "Catfish Capital of the World" because of the large size of the catfish in this part of the river! Here's an interesting tidbit—the Tennessee River runs north through Savannah. It is one of only a few rivers in the United States that does flow north.

Another way to explore the history of the town is to visit the Savannah Cemetery. Here you can visit the final resting place of famous people like Mary Elizabeth Patterson, who played Mrs. Trumbull in the I Love Lucy show, as well as Alex and Queen Haley, grandparents of famed author Alex Haley.

The beautiful, green lands and sparkling bend of the Tennessee

River whisper a sweet Southern welcome to all, and the friendly people ensure a memorable visit. As you stroll through the historic buildings of downtown, peek into the charming boutiques, and meet the friendly townspeople, we know you will love every minute of your day out in this charming Tennessee town.

PICKWICK

Blessed with some of the best fresh water fishing in the world, Pickwick, Tennessee has been called a "water sportsman's paradise." Anglers from across the United States converge on Pickwick Lake each year to try their hand at landing record catfish, sauger, crappie, white bass, striped bass, spotted bass and bluegill. The lake is absolutely breathtaking, and in the late afternoon, you will probably see some of the finest yachts in America arriving for "the season." Snowbirds from the northern areas follow the birds south via the Tennessee-Tombigbee Waterway, where you can float right up to the waterfalls for a refreshing and exciting spray. One of the best ways to see this beautiful area is on a river cruise. Rent a boat and enjoy the best the area has to offer—the crisp weather and changing color of the leaves, the sun coming up and going down over the sparkling, calm water, and a memory you will always cherish. The Pickwick Landing State Resort Park is a 1,392-acre park on the shores of Pickwick Reservoir. Here you'll find a full-service marina with dry boat storage, sailboats, wet and overnight boatslips.

The Great Outdoors

Whether you prefer sport fishing, exciting games of golf, canoeing, or just picnicking, you'll love this beautiful Tennessee oasis of fun. Fishermen can find wonderful little "fishing and hunting cabins" to rent for the season, but families flock to Pickwick Lake for unforgettable vacations and family reunions. There are many wonderful homes tucked into the banks of the river, perfect for seasonal visits.

For additional information about Savannah/Pickwick, contact the Hardin County Chamber of Commerce at 866-750-2363, 731-925-2363 or visit www.hardinchamber.org online. *(Color picture featured in front of book.)*

Savannah/Pickwick
Fairs Festivals & Fun

February
Pickwick-Hardin County
Anglers Sauger Festival

March
SJA Annual Bass Tournament
at Pickwick Lake

April
Annual Living History at
Shiloh National Military Park
Chattanooga Star Riverboat
Excursions

May
Buford Pusser Festival
Memorial Service at Shiloh
National Cemetery

June
National Catfish Derby Fishing
Rodeo
NAIA Benefit—4-Man Scramble
Golf Tournament
Lion's Club Walking Horse
Show
Annual Street Rod & Custom
Show
Education Foundation Annual
Bass Tournament

July
4th of July Extravaganza at
Pickwick
World Championship of
Catfishing Tournament
National Catfish Derby Kid's
Fishing Rodeo
Savannah Bluegrass Festival
Powerboat Superleague Races

September
Hardin County Fair
Saltillo River Day Festival
Sunset Symphony at Cherry
Mansion
Daryl Worley's Tennessee River
Run

October
Fall Foliage Driving Tours
NAIA—4-Man Scramble Golf
Tournament
Haunted Theater at the Savannah
Theater
Working Women's Luncheon

November
Davy Crockett Charity Ride

December
Victorian Christmas
Country Christmas
NAIA National Championship
Football Game

Shiloh National Military Park

Civil War history permeates this part of Tennessee, perhaps here in Hardin County more than any other location. It is best known as the site of the pivotal Civil War Battle of Shiloh. A visit to the Shiloh National Military Park at 1055 Pittsburg Landing Rd. should be first on your list of things to experience here. The park encompasses 4,000 acres overlooking the beauti-  ful Tennessee River, and it's America's best-preserved Civil War battlefield. More than 450 historic tablets, 151 monuments, and 217 cannons tell the story of The Battle of Shiloh, which was fought April 6th and 7th, 1862. Visit the Shiloh National Cemetery, the final resting-place for more than 3,500 Northern soldiers, and tour the visitor center to see an orientation film. The museum is open daily 8 am-5 pm. For more information, call 800-552-3866, 731-689-5696 or visit www.tourhardincounty.org or www.nps.gov/shil/ online.

The Cherry Mansion

Sitting high on a bluff overlooking the Tennessee River, The Cherry Mansion reigns as queen of the antebellum homes in Savannah. This beautiful home was built in 1830 by David Robinson and given to his daughter as a wedding present upon her marriage to William H. Cherry. Mr. Cherry was one of Savannah's leading merchants, who operated a shipping line on the Tennessee River. During the Civil War, the mansion served as headquarters for Major General U.S. Grant, and the lovely grounds were used as a field hospital for both Union and Confederate wounded. Mr. Bob Guinn purchased the home in 1935 and began extensive restoration. It is still privately owned by Mrs. Bob Guinn, but visitors are welcome to walk the grounds and take pictures. The Cherry Mansion, 265 W. Main St., is on the Savannah Historic District Tour. Call 800-552-3866, 731-925-8181, or visit www.tourhardincounty.org online.

Tennessee River Museum

Chronicling prehistoric times, life of the Mississippian Mound Builders, the tragic story of the "Trail of Tears," the Civil War, the Golden Age of Steamboats, and the mighty Tennessee River as it is today, Savannah's Tennessee River Museum is a wonderful tribute to this unique area.

Located at 507 Main St. in the old post office building, the Tennessee River Museum features displays depicting life along the lower Tennessee River Valley, including archaeology, paleontology, and musseling. You'll see the replica steamboat pilothouse and the famed Shiloh Effigy Pipe that was uncovered in 1898 at Shiloh National Military Park. This pipe is one of the finest Indian relics ever discovered! The Tennessee River Museum is open Monday-Saturday 9 am-5 pm and Sunday 1-5 pm. For more information, call 800-552-3866, 731-925-2364, or visit www.tourhardincounty.org online.

Savannah Historic District Walking/Driving Tours

If you want to truly experience the incredible history of a sweet Southern town, take a Savannah Historic District Walking/Driving Tour. The two-mile drive or stroll takes you past 17 historic homes, depicting the several architectural styles of the area. All of the historic homes are privately owned, and some have been historically restored. You'll see the famous Cherry Mansion, headquarters for General U.S. Grant during the Civil War, The First Presbyterian Church, which was used as a hospital for Union troops, and the beautiful Trail of Tears overlook. You can also explore the Tennessee River Museum and Hardin County Convention and Visitors Bureau that was once the old post office building. Experience stepping back into a 19th century river town where you can walk in a century-old atmosphere and listen to the whispers of history. Call 800-552-3866, 731-925-8181, or visit www.tourhardincounty.org online.

PICKWICK LAKE VACATION RENTALS

Imagine a family vacation or a reunion in a beautiful waterfront home with outdoor hot tub, private boat/swim dock, and panoramic view of three states! You can have all this, a cozy cabin nestled in the trees, or even a luxury condo at Grand Harbor. Call Beverly Glover at Pickwick Lake Vacation Rentals, 800-848-8177, 11268 Hwy. 57 E, for the perfect vacation getaway. Open 9am-5pm Monday-Saturday. For additional info on cabins visit www.pickwicklakecabins.com online.

Whether you desire a tucked away cabin on the river, an elegant lake house, or a home just steps from the golf course, the agents at Crunk Real Estate, 890 Pickwick St. in Savannah know just the place. They are experts in the West Tennessee area. Visit www.crunkrealestate.com online, or call 800-243-8818, 731-925-4433.

GREENE'S FINE ANTIQUES & INTERIOR DESIGNS

While visiting the friendly, Southern town of Savannah, you must stop by Greene's Fine Antiques & Interior Designs. Millie Greene opened her decorating business in 1989, becoming a first choice interior designer for Savannah and Pickwick Lake residents. She travels to High Point and Atlanta to find extraordinary items for her clients, and she carries a remarkable selection of unique gift items. You'll find the latest furniture from Henredon, Barcalounger, Parker Southern, Hickory Chair and more, as well as the most beautiful china and crystal patterns from Vietri, Present Tense, Pickard, Lenox and others. You'll love the special soaps, lotions, and bath gels, and the delicious home fragrances and candles from Aromatique. Greene's Fine Antiques & Interior Designs, 4070 Wayne Rd. is open Monday–Saturday 10 am-5 pm. For more information, call 731-925-5586.

BURT'S INC.

Family-owned-and-operated by the Burgess' since 1961, Burt's Inc. continues to meet the home décor needs of Savannah and the surrounding area. The newly expanded showroom displays furnishings by Broyhill, Lane, Ashley, and BenchCraft. Burt's also carries appliances from GE, Maytag and Fisher & Paykel. Stop by Monday-Friday 8 am-5:30 pm or Saturday until 5 pm at 2312 Wayne Rd. and let David or Dennis take care of your furniture and appliance needs. To learn more, call 731-925-2554.

Gifts & Home Décor

So, how shall we describe Eclectic Spaces? Well, Ann Stafford has brought together "uncommon things for comfortable living," "ideas to light up your life," and "accessories to reflect the aspects of your personality!" Located at 11256 Hwy. 57 in Pickwick, this beautiful store is filled to the brim with accessories. Open Monday-Saturday 10 am-5 pm and Sunday noon-5 pm in the summer. Visit www.pickwickshopping.com or call 731-689-4455 to learn more.

Hotels

DAYS INN OF SAVANNAH

You will discover sweet little surprises during your stay at the Days Inn of Savannah, 1695 Pickwick Rd. The first surprise? The genuine warmth and friendliness of the management greets you with a smile. Surprise number two? A delicious continental breakfast is served each morning in the breakfast room. Surprise number three? There's a wonderful swimming pool for the guest's enjoyment. The very clean and pretty rooms include coffee makers, blow dryers, and color TVs. There are microwave and refrigerator rooms available on a first come basis and irons and ironing boards are available at the front desk. Call 731-925-5505, toll free 800-DAYS INN, or visit www.daysinn.com.

"Located in the Famous Pickwick Curve"

"Probably the best ribs you'll ever eat," that's what they say about The Rib Cage of Pickwick. Savory Southern pit bar-b-que awaits you at 12840 Hwy. 57 S.—just look for the red tin roof. In the famous Pickwick Curve, The Rib Cage welcomes you in a bathing suit or a business suit. Dine on the patio or inside. Catering is available, and they'll even package your ribs, chicken or chops for the boat. Stop by Sunday-Thursday 10 am-9 pm and Friday-Saturday 10 am-10 pm. Call 731-689-3637.

You'll feel as though you are on a tropical island instead of in a small Tennessee town when you visit Freddy T's Restaurant and "Beach Club" on Pickwick Lake at 12750 Hwy. 57 S. in Pickwick. You'll enjoy delicious seafood dishes, a game room for kiddos, live entertainment, two bars, and a fabulous atmosphere out back at The Beach Club! For special nights, limo service is available. The restaurant is open Monday-Saturday at 5 pm and the beach club Thursday-Saturday at 8 pm. Call 731-689-3099.

Index

Cross Reference

Yarrow Acres – 193

Hotels / Motels

Baymont Inn & Suites – Cookeville – 143

Baymont Inn & Suites – Franklin – 197

Baymont Inn & Suites – Goodlettsville – 222, XII

Best Western Fayetteville Inn & Trotters Restaurant – 173

Comfort Inn – Dickson – 156

Comfort Suites – Lebanon – 240

Country Hearth Inn – 172

Courtyard Marriott – Chattanooga – 79, X

Courtyard Marriott Vanderbilt – Nashville – 45

Days Inn of Savannah – 264

Gaylord Opryland Resort & Convention – 43, Front Cover

Hampton Inn – Columbia – 230

Hampton Inn & Suites – Franklin – 198

Jameson Inn – 222

Lynchburg Country Inn – 172

Magnolia House Bed & Breakfast – 187

Red Roof Inns – 96

Richland Inns – 230

The Hermitage Hotel – 45

Union Station – A Wyndham Historic Hotel – 44

Ice Cream Parlors

Bluebird Antiques & Ice Cream Parlour – 88

Clumpies Ice Cream Co. – 78

Interior Design

Bedroom Elegance / Betty Jane Interiors – 46

Bella Linea – 47

Bradford's – 24

Brentwood Interiors – 95

Circa Home Interiors LLC – 191, XI

Cousins – 114

Custom Creations – 221

Dumpster Divers Antiques – 249

Gilchrist Gilchrist – 28

Greene's Fine Antiques & Interior Designers – 263

Happiness Place – 42

Katydid's – 182

Maitland's – 48

Northgate Gallery, Inc. – Chattanooga (Hixson) – 66

Patricia Jane & Company – 219

ReCreations – 26, VII

Ro's Oriental Rugs, Inc. – 48

Serendipity – 38

SGO Designer Glass – 253

Simply Brigitte – 106

The Iron Gate – 181

Jewelry

Along the Way – 183

Anna Ball White – 71

Berenice Denton's Estate Sales & Appraisals / B. Denton's Cottage – 29

Blest Friends Boutique – 155

Body, Mind & Spirit, Inc. – 106

Busy Beads & Moore – 108

Carter's Drug Store – 171

Cherie's Unique Collections – 196

Churches Antiques & Estate Pieces and Mountain City Realtors – 68

Cindi Earl – 49

Colleen's Cottage – 170

Cousins – 114

Cuz's Antique Center – 236

Elite Repeats – 139

Elizabeth Gregory, LLC – 97

Enjoué – 190

Fischer Evans – 80

For Every Child – 189

Heritage Jewelers – 173

Jamie, Inc – 36

Jensen Travelwear by Jacqueline – 39

Jerry Lindsey – 98

JJ Jax – 132

Jo Ann's – 153

Lambs & Ivy – 69

Madison Ave. Boutique – 107

Memory Makers – 105

Merchant's Walk on Main – 166

Miss Martha's Mercantile – 153

Mole Hill Pottery – 69

Plaid Rabbit – 189

Prissy's – 170

Robin's Boutique – 139

Serendipity – 38

Shelton's – 144

Dear Adventurer,

If you are reading this book chances are you are an 'Adventurer.' An 'Adventurer' is a person with a sense of adventure and a curiosity for new and exciting places, people and experiences—both long and short distances. All of the Lady's Day Out books appeal to that sense of adventure and cater to the natural curiosity in all of us.

A Lady's Day Out, Inc., would like to share this gift of the perfect combination between work and travel with our loyal following of readers.

In an effort to expand our coverage area we are looking for adventurous travelers who would like to help us find the greatest places to include in our upcoming editions of A Lady's Day Out. This is a wonderful opportunity to travel and explore some of the best destination cities in the United States.

If you would like more information, we would love to hear from you. You may call A Lady's Day Out, Inc. at 1-888-860-ALDO (2536) or e-mail us through www.aladysdayout.com online.

Best wishes and keep on exploring, from all of us at A Lady's Day Out, Inc.

"A Lady's Day Out Giveaway" Entry Form

Have five of the businesses featured in this book sign your entry form and you are eligible to win one of the following: weekend get away at a bed and breakfast, dinner gift certificates, shopping spree gift certificates or $250 cash.

1. _____
   (NAME OF BUSINESS)   (SIGNATURE)

2. _____
   (NAME OF BUSINESS)   (SIGNATURE)

3. _____
   (NAME OF BUSINESS)   (SIGNATURE)

4. _____
   (NAME OF BUSINESS)   (SIGNATURE)

5. _____
   (NAME OF BUSINESS)   (SIGNATURE)

NAME: _____

ADDRESS: _____

CITY: _____ STATE: _____ ZIP: _____

PHONE#: _____ E-MAIL: _____

Where did you purchase book? _____

Other towns or businesses you feel should be incorporated in our next book. _____
_____

No purchase necessary. Winners will be determined by random drawing from all complete entries received. Winners will be notified by phone and/or mail.

Mail To:
A Lady's Day Out, Inc.
8563 Boat Club Road
Fort Worth, Tx 76179

Fax To:
817-236-0033
Phone: 817-236-5250
Web-Site: www.aladysdayout.com

NOTES

NOTES